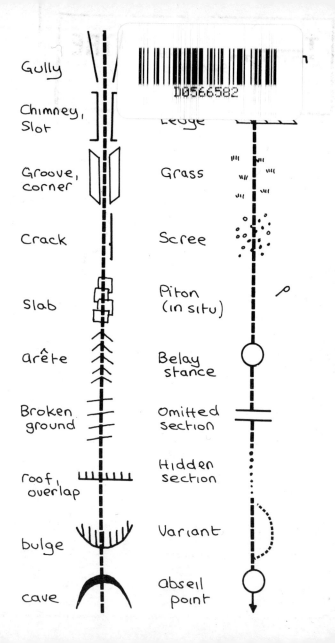

Gully			
Chimney, Slot		Ledge	
Groove, corner		Grass	
Crack		Scree	
Slab		Piton (in situ)	
arête		Belay stance	
Broken ground		Omitted section	
roof, overlap		Hidden section	
bulge		Variant	
cave		abseil point	

St Helens
College
Library

4.99

100 CLASSIC CLIMBS

YORKSHIRE AND THE PEAK DISTRICT

Limestone

The Crowood Press

First published in 1991 by
The Crowood Press Ltd
Gipsy Lane
Swindon
Wiltshire SN2 6DQ

British Library Cataloguing in Publication Data
Jackson, Chris
  100 classic climbs: Yorkshire and the Peak District, limestone.
  1. England. Peak district 2. Yorkshire. Limestone
  regions. Rock climbing
  I. Title
  796.52230942511

ISBN 1–85223–319–2

Acknowledgements

I would like to thank my wife, Suzy, for allowing herself to become
a 'Book Widow' over the last eighteen months, and also Ian Smith,
Bill Wintrip and Simon Waller for helping me with the proof reading.

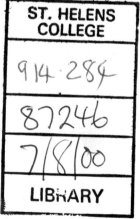
Typeset by Input Typesetting Ltd, London, SW19 8DR
Printed in Great Britain by BPCC Hazell Books Ltd, Aylesbury

Contents

Preface

100 Classic Climbs on Peak and Pennine Limestone describes a wide selection of all that is best on the limestone crags of the Peak District and the Yorkshire Dales. In this guide, topo diagrams take the place of the usual written route descriptions while the accompanying text gives information on such topics as approaches, best conditions and where to stay. More intimate details of the route, such as atmosphere and history, are also given, along with tips and comments on how to get up and down.

Worldwide, topos are becoming increasingly popular as a means of describing the line of a route, the pictoral format has become standardized and is able to convey a degree of information which would be laborious in text form.

Although the book is entitled *100 Classic Climbs*, there are in fact almost 150 routes described because in many instances several routes have been grouped together under one heading, usually when they are in close proximity to one another. Selecting these routes has not been easy and I often felt that *1000 Classic Climbs* might be more appropriate.

Limestone is a fertile rock, and I make no apology for only including two routes below VS because most of the easier routes, and limestone does not have many, are often grassy, crumbly and difficult to protect – a veritable botanist's paradise. At VS and above, the routes become steeper and cleaner. Slabs are uncommon, certainly on Peak limestone, and usually the degree of strenuousness of the climb increases with its grade. Protection is generally good as much limestone is well cracked and faulted, although a certain amount of ingenuity is sometimes required to arrange protection around pockets and natural threads which occur on certain crags. Grades therefore range between VS and E3; the actual distribution is shown in the accompanying bar chart. Classic extremes in the Peak District and Yorkshire Dales extend well beyond the E3 category but their inclusion in a guide book of this type seemed inappropriate and I have made the upper limit E3 6a.

As with Steve Ashton's previous guide books in this series, I have attempted to ensure that no area contains too few routes to give a good day's climbing. I hope that you like my selection. Some routes are obvious classics, some not so obvious and others just favourites of mine. Good climbing.

Climbing on Peak and Pennine Limestone

Limestone forms much of the lowland scenery in the Peak District and many of the crags are situated amidst lush vegetation, often within popular beauty spots. Broadly, the crags fall into two categories: valley crags such as in Chee Dale and Dovedale, and the escarpments such as High Tor and Wildcat Crags. The valley crags, with the exception of Stoney Middleton Dale, are generally slow to dry out and the narrow limestone valleys sometimes prevent the sun ever reaching them in the winter months. Chee Tor suffers from this problem but not all valley crags are out of condition in the soggy winter months; Beeston Tor can be a sun trap even in the depths of January.

Stoney Middleton is perhaps the most popular meeting place for limestone climbing in the north of The Peak. It sports the Lovers' Leap Café, usually referred to as 'Stoney Caf', has an excellent crag in close proximity which dries quickly and for those with transport is fairly close to other crags in the Wye Valley such as Chee Tor and Water-cum-Jolly.

For those wishing to be gently introduced into the delights of limestone climbing, Ravensdale perhaps offers the best option. Set in a superb position on the valley rim there are some fine multi-pitch VSs and HVSs worthy of any visiting party.

Along the Wye Valley the crags tend to be steep and pocketed. The most popular crag here must be Chee Tor, and rightly so, as almost every route warrants classic status though it can be very busy once it comes into condition. For those requiring a quieter venue, Water-cum-Jolly offers some good climbing in idyllic situations along the banks of the River Wye. Perhaps a little overshadowed by the quality of the routes further upstream in Chee Dale, the valley remains one of my favourites.

In the south of The Peak, there are two main areas, Matlock and Dovedale/Manifold. High Tor at Matlock is probably The Peak's premier crag, with routes to suit a wide range of abilities, perfect rock, splendid positions and a café on the summit. Somewhat less intimidating but well worth a visit are the nearby Wildcat Crags and Willersley Castle Rocks.

For those with a penchant for exploration, there are the delights of Dovedale, a wonderful collection of ridges and spires set along the banks of the beautiful but very popular River Dove. Running roughly parallel with Dovedale is the Manifold Valley, a much more peaceful place, possibly because there is no convenient through route for walking parties or because the river chooses a subterranean path in all but the wettest weather. Here there is the superb Beeston Tor, a virtual all-the-year-round crag, and the imposing but draughty Thor's Cave.

In the Yorkshire Dales, with the exception of Gordale Scar, the crags tend to be escarpments. The prime crag in the Dales has to be Malham Cove. This contains the highest concentration of quality limestone routes in the area, with numerous classics ranging from VS to E3. This huge amphitheatre is a very popular tourist spot, with the boys on the bolts on the overhanging back wall elevating (or reducing?) climbing into spectator sport status. Close to Malham is Gordale Scar and the superb Face Route – a dramatic gorge though usually regarded as a summer crag as it can be somewhat draughty and prone to seepage.

In the west side of the Dales is Crummackdale, which contains some excellent and unusual slab routes on prickly, pocketed limestone in an idyllic setting. To the east, Kilnsey Crag is probably the second best-known piece of rock in the Dales, the classic Diedre is a 'must', and after that, the nearby Loup Scar which overhangs the River Wharfe should keep you occupied until the pubs open.

As a rough indication of the state of the various crags throughout the months of the year, I have attempted to produce a quick reference table which should offer some guidance to a visiting party. As with most rules there will be exceptions: in a dry winter virtually all the crags may be in condition although some may be cold and never see the sun. Indeed, during the preparation of this guide, many of the traditional summer crags were dry until the middle of December. However, if there is a wet summer certain crags may remain out of condition for most of the year.

How to use the Guide

AREA AND CRAG INTRODUCTIONS

In the Peak District, routes are described within 6 main areas: Stoney Middleton, Ravensdale, Chee Dale, Water-cum-Jolly, the Matlock area, Dovedale and the Manifold Valley. The descriptions include approaches by car or by public transport, where to stay and where to obtain services etc. An accompanying map identifies approaches and parking areas. Where there are several crags within an area and access or approach is complicated, a detailed description is given for each crag. Crag diagrams are given where possible to help identification of a particular buttress. Chee Tor and Willersley Castle Rocks are absent because the density of the tree cover prevented any suitable perspective for drawing. Here, a plan diagram has been used to help identify the starting points of the routes. The Yorkshire Dales are covered in three main areas: Malham Cove, which contains the lion's share of classic routes, the Western Crags and the Eastern Crags.

ROUTE INFORMATION

Concise details of each route are presented under six headings.

Summary: A concise description of the route, with comments on its quality and any salient features. The title gives the route length and its adjectival grade.

First Ascents: Brief historical details. On limestone, many routes were originally aided and therefore first ascents and first free ascents are given.

Best Conditions: Along with the quick reference diagram, this helps you to select a suitable crag for the season and the prevailing weather.

Approach: Gets you to the crag by the easiest route, with details such as parking and approach time. Grid references are given for each crag.

Starting Point: Locates the start of the route and the beginning of the topo which is then used for all further description of the route. The starting point description should be used in conjunction with the crag diagram or plan which shows the route number.

Descent: Note that a few descents are by abseil only; unless otherwise marked, a double 45m rope should be adequate.

ROUTE DESCRIPTIONS

This is not essential reading for route-finding on the crags but rather a few general notes and comments, as well as the odd tip.

TOPO DIAGRAMS

All routes are identified by a number between 1 and 100 which is used on topos in the text and on crag diagrams. Topos replace the conventional written route descriptions. There is a diagram explaining the topo symbols at the front of the guide. Many of the topos have been drawn from photographs so the scale of the pitches and features on the pitches should be reasonably accurate. However, foreshortening occurs in photographs and it is not possible to represent every twist and turn of a route with a dotted line. Therefore, topos are best used in conjunction with intuitive route-finding.

Many topos show groups of several routes when they are close together, the number on the route line relates to the description number. Where several routes are described under one heading, these will all have the same number but may be separately identified by the initials of the route name. Occasionally, a worthwhile neighbouring route is indicated by dotted line and grade, the absence of a route number indicates that no description is given.

GRADINGS

The normal adjectival grades have been given throughout the guide. Technical grades are given on the topos and, where possible, the crux of the route is indicated. The range of grades and their international equivalents are as follows:

British Adjectival Grade		Technical	UIAA	USA	France
S	Severe	4a–4b	IV+	5.6	5a–5b
VS	Very Severe	4b–5a	V+	5.7	5a–5c
HVS	Hard Very Severe	4c–5b	VI	5.9	5b–6a
E1	Extreme	5a–5c	VI+	5.10a/b	6a–6b
E2	Extreme	5b–6a	VII	5.10c/d	6b–6c
E3	Extreme	5b–6b	VII+	5.11a/b	6b–7a

Interpreting Grades: The first column in the table shows the overall or adjectival grade. This takes into account everything which might make the route difficult. Reasons include seriousness, sustained nature of climbing and poor protection. The technical grade gives purely the technical difficulty of a move, how thin, strenuous or gymnastic it is. A combination of the two grades gives a good indication of the type of climbing to be expected on a route. For example, E1 5a would suggest that the technicality of the move is not high but it may be badly protected, very sustained or on poor rock, or have some other factor that pushes up its stopping power. Conversely, an HVS 5c route contains a hard move but it is either very well protected or is perhaps the first move off the ground.

ACCESS

Almost without exception, crags within this guide lie on private land and though public rights of way may pass close to some of the crags there is rarely any right to climb on them. Currently, there are few problems of access but landowners and their attitudes can change and climbers are asked to respond to any confrontation with discretion and courtesy. Abuse will cause difficulties for us all. Any problems of this nature should be referred to the British Mountaineering Council, Crawford House, Precinct Centre, Booth Street East, Manchester M13 9RZ. Tel: 061 273 5835.

FURTHER INFORMATION

For further information on campsites and accommodation in the Peak District, contact The East Midlands Tourist Board, Exchequergate, Lincoln, LN2 1PZ. Tel: 0522 531521 or The Peak District National Park, Aldern House, Baslow Road, Bakewell, Derbyshire DE4 1AE. Tel: 062 981 4321. For the Yorkshire Dales, contact The Yorkshire Dales National Park, 32 Tarn Moor, Skipton, Yorkshire, BD23 1LT. Tel: 0756 794296.

Maps: The Peak District is best covered by the 1:25 000 Outdoor Leisure Map 24 (White Peak Area). For the Yorkshire Dales, Crummackdale is covered by the 1:25 000 Yorkshire Dales Outdoor Leisure Map 2 (Western Area), and the other crags by the Yorkshire Dales (Southern Area) Outdoor Leisure Map 10.

Guidebooks: Milburn, G., (ed), *Peak District Climbs* (in three volumes) (British Mountaineering Council, 1987).
Desroy, G., (ed), *Yorkshire Limestone* (Yorkshire Limestone Guidebook Steering Committee for the Yorkshire Mountaineering Council, 1987).

DISTRIBUTION OF GRADES

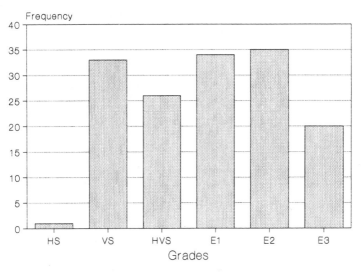

A FINAL CAUTIONARY NOTE

Route information in this guide is based on notes and sketches made while at the crag or shortly afterwards. All the routes have been climbed or reclimbed in the last two years, most within the last twelve months and every effort has been made to ensure the accuracy of the topo diagrams. Inevitably there will be disagreements as to the exact line of a route and its level of difficulty. Routes also change; limestone is quite prone to having pieces break off, large and small, trees die or are broken and ledges collapse. If the error is on my part then I apologize in advance. If you do experience any difficulty or have any comments on the guide, then please write to Chris Jackson, care of The Crowood Press Ltd. I would be very grateful and your help in updating the guide would be acknowledged in future editions.

Stoney Middleton
Ravensdale
Chee Dale Plum Buttress
              Chee Tor
Water-cum-Jolly R bank
                  L bank
Matlock   Pic Tor
              High Tor
              Wildcat
              Willersley
Dovedale   Ravens Tor
              Baley Buttress
              Ilam Rock
              Pickering O/H
              Watchblock
              Tissington S.
              Dovedale Ch.
Manifold V. Thor's Cave
              Beeston Tor

Malham Cove
Gordale Scar
Kilnsey Crag
Loup Scar
Crummackdale

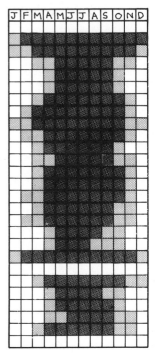

	usually out of condition
	sometimes in condition
	usually in condition

Stoney Middleton Area

The cliffs of Stoney Middleton hold a special place in the heart of many limestone climbers for it was these cliffs that were the forcing ground for much of the limestone climbing in the Peak District during the 1960s and early 1970s. A combination of easy access, good pubs, accommodation and the essential café created a catalyst for exploration and route development. Since then, much of the world has caught up. However, Stoney Café remains the same, an essential institution, offering food and drink to the weary, argument to the jaded and shelter in times of storm.

Approaches: Stoney Middleton cliffs flank the north side of the A623 road west of the village, 24km south of Sheffield and 9km north of Bakewell. The T208 bus service from Sheffield to Buxton and Hanley passes through the dale and the 240 bus from Sheffield to Bakewell stops at Calver Sough, 1km east of Stoney Middleton Village. From Chesterfield, buses go to Baslow where connections can be made. From Manchester, the most practical route is to Bakewell, via Buxton.

Accommodation: Camping – there are no official sites close to the crags, although the Promenade will accommodate a few tents. If camping here, **please take your litter home**, do not leave the crags looking like a rubbish tip. Further afield, there is the Eric Byne campsite near Baslow, off the A619 at SK 277727, and camping close to Hope Village at SK 174833 and by the Plough Inn, Hathersage, at SK 235805.
Bivouacs – there is a suitable site on Windy Ledge.
Youth hostels – at Buxton, Eyam, Bretton, Hathersage and Ravenstor.
Hotels, b. & b. – available at numerous pubs and hotels in the area.

Services: There are post offices in Stoney Middleton, Eyam and Calver and petrol stations 200m west of Stoney Café and in Calver. The Moon in Stoney Middleton is a popular meeting place, as is The Royal Oak and several pubs in Eyam. Eyam has several shops, a chippy and toilets. Stoney Middleton has two village stores and sometimes a chippy. There are public telephones in Stoney Middleton and in Eyam. There is parking 100m west of the café, just outside the village and the tracks up to the crag can be driven at some risk to the underside of your vehicle.

A Concise History: The first climbers to venture on to the cliffs of Stoney Middleton were probably J. W. Puttrell and Henry Bishop at some time prior to 1910. Unfortunately records were not kept of their exploits. Eric Byne and Clifford Moyer also visited the crags in about 1933, climbing several routes, but again there seem to be no surviving records of the climbs. During the 1940s and 1950s, members of the Valkyrie Club, including Joe Brown and friends, put up several new routes but it was not until about 1957 that any serious development of the crag was undertaken. Between 1957 and 1961, Dave Johnson, Trevor Brooks, Jack Wade, and John and Brenda Salt made repeated visits to Stoney Middleton, and later Dave Mellor and Dave Johnson together initiated climbing on Windy Buttress but, as with many of the steeper ascents in those days, a considerable amount of aid was used.

The next phase of development started after the publishing of 'The Little Blue Book', Graham West's *Rock Climbs on the Mountain Limestone of Derbyshire* in 1961. Climbers such as Jack Street, Dave Nowill, Chris Jackson, Geoff Birtles and others, banded together into what later became the Cioch Club, and for several years during the sixties they occupied the upper room at the end of the cottages which contain the café. These climbers found that they had the crags virtually to themselves as there were few other climbers about. Most regarded limestone as dangerous stuff, a situation unknown in today's busy scene. The Cioch or 'The Stoney Mob' as they were often known made their mark on most of the Peak District's limestone crags during that period and many of the modern classics at Stoney Middleton were discovered by these climbers during those ten years.

The 1970s were probably the summer years in the development of Stoney Middleton. During this period, Tom Proctor and Gabriel Regan were perhaps the leading lights amongst many, eliminating aid from many existing 'mixed' routes and initiating some of the hardest routes on limestone at the time.

Since then there have been a few major new lines climbed and many fillers-in; almost all are hard and some, such as Jerry Moffat's The Little Plum, still see very few repeats. Future years will no doubt see the gaps closing still further as standards continue to rise.

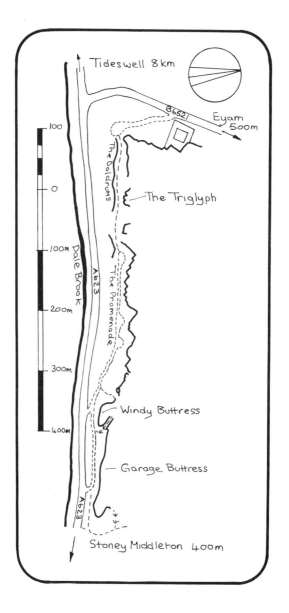

1: PENDULUM (HVS) 90m

Summary: A striking line, taking a prominent horizontal break which crosses Garage Buttress at two-thirds height. The route traverses into some impressive situations but always at a reasonable grade with excellent protection. Some parties forsake the final pitch for the top pitch of Rippemoff (3) which is slightly easier. A good selection of larger nuts and camming devices may be found useful for protection.

First Ascent: Brian Moore and Pete Fieldsend in 1963, as an aid route. The frequent failure of numerous wooden wedges gave the route its name. It was subsequently climbed free by Jack Street and Chris Jackson.

Best Conditions: Garage Buttress faces south but the break is susceptible to some weeping after prolonged wet spells, particularly the last pitch. The route is fairly sheltered however, and can make an excellent outing, especially on a sunny winter's day.

Approach: *See* Approaches under Stoney Middleton. From the village, follow the A623 westwards for 500m. Garage Buttress is the first crag beyond the garage and is characterized by a break at two-thirds height.

Starting Point: At the right end of the break. To reach this, take the track up the hillside and traverse left once the appropriate altitude has been reached.

Descent: At the end of pitch 3, climb down or lower off tat to a ledge and traverse left to some trees. The second climber can normally arrange a back rope through *in situ* gear and be belayed down by the leader. From the trees, abseil to the ground. For those taking the Rippemoff finish, *see* the descent for that route (3).

The break can be hand jammed in many places although plentiful small holds on the outer edge of the break make for more elegant climbing. The first pitch eases for a while as it rounds a broad arête, luring you into a false sense of security but one step around the corner and the exposure comes up to grab you again. The traverse passes under the overhangs of The Little Plum, one of Stoney's hardest routes, and crosses into a shallow corner where the crack closes up. The next couple of moves look intimidating, the rock cuts away below and it is not possible to see around the arête. However, protection abounds and, once round, the crack opens up again and easier moves lead to another arête, The Saddle. This feature was once much larger than it is now and could be sat astride. Alas, years of gravity and climbers have reduced it to its current state.

The last pitch of The Pendulum has a different character from the first two. The crack closes down and becomes intermittent, requiring some strenuous moves before easier ground is reached.

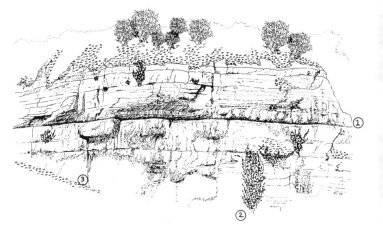

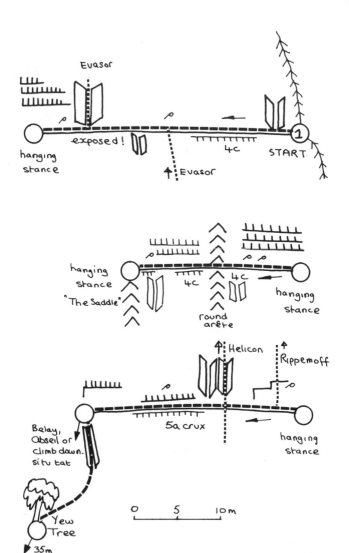

Evasor

hanging
stance

exposed!

Evasor

4c

START

1

hanging
stance

"The Saddle"

round
arête

4c

4c

hanging
stance

Helicon

Rippemoff

5a crux

hanging
stance

Belay,
Obseil or
Climb down.
situat

Yew
Tree

35m

0   5   10m

Bob Bradley on Highlight (Route 43), High Tor, Matlock. (Photo: Chris Jackson.)

2: EVASOR (VS) 45m

Summary: Probably the most exposed VS on limestone. From mediocre beginnings, the route traverses in a tremendous position into the airy finishing groove.

First Ascent: Paul Nunn and M. Richardson in January 1965, using 5 points of aid. Loose rock was progressively removed and the route was soon freed.

Best Conditions: The start can retain a little dampness but the rest faces south and dries quickly.

Approach: *See* Approaches under Stoney Middleton area. From the village, follow the A623 westward for 500m. Garage Buttress is the first crag beyond the garage and is characterized by a break at two-thirds height.

Starting Point: Some 20m right of the drive way, at the foot of a broad arête leading to a small ash tree.

Descent: Traverse right (facing in) along the prickly summit slope until it is possible to climb through bushes to a steep descent path leading to a small valley.

The route traverses into sensational positions usually only found on the 'E' grade routes. From a cosy stance behind a small tree, the sense of exposure rapidly increases as one creeps along the break taken by The Pendulum (1). Once in a standing position in the small groove, jugs immediately come to hand and it is pure exhilaration all the way to the top.

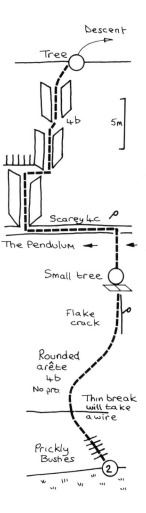

3: RIPPEMOFF & HELICON (E1, E2)
22m, 30m

Summary: Steep and exhilarating climbing up thin cracks towards the left end of Garage Buttress. The first pitch is common to both routes but Rippemoff nips off right at the break to belay and to take an easier line to the top. Helicon is best led out in one long pitch. The rock is good and protection is excellent.

First Ascent: Rippemoff – Chris Jackson and Geoff Birtles in 1965, using 2 points of aid and later freed by Keith Myhill. Helicon – originally climbed as an aid route by Bob Dearman and Graham Hawker in 1963, freed in 1970 by Jack Street and Paul Nunn.

Best Conditions: The routes face south, and are rarely wet.

Approach: *See* Approaches under Stoney Middleton area. From the village, follow the A623 westward for 500m. Garage Buttress is the first crag beyond the garage and is characterized by a break at two-thirds height.

Starting Point: The left flank of Garage Buttress contains a rising grass bank at about one-third height. The routes start from the right end of this, close to a patch of ivy. Scramble up past trees to a ledge with *in situ* belay pegs.

Descent: The top of the climb is a bank of grass and roses, backed by thorn bushes. Traverse to the right (facing in) to a gap in the bushes which overlooks the end of the buttress. Scramble down through trees into an easy descent valley. It is possible to abseil to the deck on double 50m ropes from trees at the top of the routes.

The first 10m lead fairly easily into a black slot below a bulge where protection is good, but the peg above has been driven in so far that there is little room for a karabiner so it is usually threaded by an *in situ* sling. Above the bulge there are sharp holds and it takes just two moves to regain the vertical and reach a huge thread runner in the break. Here the routes divide. Rippemoff traverses right to a peg belay on The Saddle, then moves back left to climb a wall above, on perfect rock, via a thin crack line and a small gorse bush. From the thread runner in the break, Helicon climbs the right-hand groove above. The start is tricky but it is possible to keep the protection above your head and better holds arrive at a deep crack which takes excellent runners. Above, the rock steepens and, beyond a peg runner, further protection is difficult to arrange, more so because of the steepness. Do not move left into the adjacent groove to gain a prominent runner placement as the move back above this is difficult and the runner usually lifts out anyway. A series of 'balancy' moves between sharp holds leads to the finishing jugs in superb position.

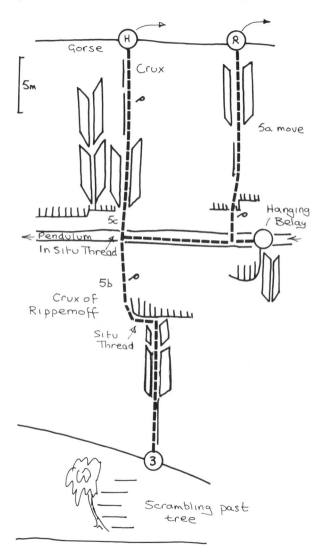

Gorse

H   Crux

R

5a move

5m

5c

Hanging / Belay

Pendulum
In Situ Thread

5b

Crux of
Rippemoff

Situ
Thread

3

Scrambling past
tree

WINDY BUTTRESS

Windy Buttress contains some of Stoney Middleton's finest routes. The buttress is difficult to miss, being approximately 50m high and almost overhanging the A623 about 100m west of the garage. The most prominent feature is the huge stepped overhang on the front face which is taken by The Flakes (8). The right edge of this face is the arête of Windhover, and right again is the hugh concavity containing Scoop Wall (7). The right edge of the buttress is a fine arête, around from which is the top pitch of Aurora (5). Left of The Flakes, the face drops back below a jungle-filled gully and then increases in height before finishing at a prominent crack line taken by Inquisitor (E1 5c).

At half height, Windy Buttress is girdled by Windy Ledge, a remarkable ledge system inherited from the ancient lead miners. The ledge can be gained from the left end of the Buttress and gives access to many of the routes. The ledge runs around the arête of Windhover and ends at a widening below Scoop Wall. Further progress can only be achieved by a V. Diff traverse at hand level, Tiger Trot, which leads to the belay at the top of pitch 1 of Aurora and the termination of the ledge in the descent gully.

Left of Windhover is Key Hole Cave, which leads through Windy Buttress to the descent gully via a very twisty hands and knees crawl (traditionally undertaken after closing hours and without lights).

4: ALCASAN (E2) 135m

Summary: One of Stoney Middleton's classic expeditions, traversing Windy Buttress from right to left in a tremendous position. The route starts up Aurora and traverses the whole of Windy Buttress to finish at the top of Inquisitor. The difficulties are well balanced, with no single pitch being excessively harder than the rest. Much of the protection is from *in situ* pegs; a selection of small to medium wires will be found useful.

First Ascent: Bob Dearman and Brian Moore crossed from Aurora to the end of The Flakes, using a considerable amount of direct aid, in 1964. Chris Jackson and Jim Ballard soon repeated this section using only 1 point of aid. The final section from The Flakes to Inquisitor was achieved by Jackson and Moore in late 1964, using 2 points of aid to gain the corner of Kellog.

Best Conditions: The route faces south and gets all the available sun. Drainage is minimal, although the stretch between the corner of Kellog and the start of the final wall can hold a little dampness after a prolonged wet spell.

Approach: *See* introductory notes for Windy Buttress.

Starting Point: Below Windy Buttress is a huge square corner taken by the first pitch of Memnon (6) Alcasan starts right of this at the foot of a polished crack and a corner system.

Descent: The best method of descent is by abseil from any of the suitable trees. However, it is possible to press on upwards through the rose bushes to the flat, grassy summit of Windy Buttress. From here, the descent is as for Route 5.

At first sight, the traverse across Scoop Wall to Windhover arête is intimidating. However, once committed, good holds soon come to hand. Perfect rock on the first section becomes slightly suspect as one traverses out towards the arête of Windhover although, technically, the climbing is a little easier. Alternatives present themselves from the tiny stance on Windhover. It is possible to traverse left across Armageddon and swing down in sickening position into the top of The Flakes, or to climb down until you are able to traverse as for The Flakes. Either way presents superb climbing. Good rope work will prevent serious rope drag at this stage. As with any traverse, the leader should always remember the second and, if possible, place protection after a difficult section as well as before it.

   The technical crux of the route is the traverse into Kellog. The leader is presented with a descending traverse from a hanging arête into the prominent corner of Kellog. It is possible for the second climber to arrange a back rope through fixed gear, providing that double ropes are being used. The final wall becomes progressively thinner until the wide crack of Inquisitor is reached.

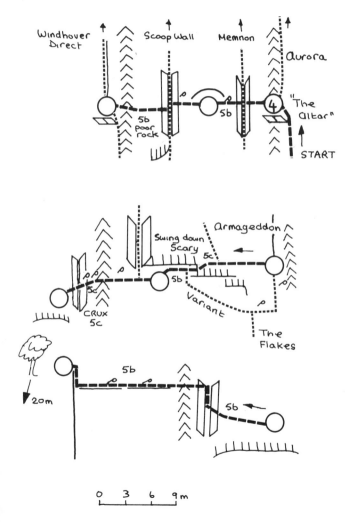

5: AURORA (VS) 51m

Summary: The easiest route up Windy Buttress, culminating in a position of tremendous exposure where the route steps left just below the top. The first pitch weaves a devious line up the broad toe of the arête which bounds the right-hand side of Windy Buttress. In contrast, the second pitch follows a striking corner to the right of the arête. Protection on the lower pitch is adequate and on the upper pitch, more than adequate.

First Ascent: F. Elliott in 1933 and called The Great Ridge. It was an ascent many years ahead of its time and was featured in the *Sheffield Telegraph*. Probably only the top pitch was climbed; no record remains of the first ascent of the lower section of the route.

Best Conditions: At any time. The second pitch may retain a little dampness after a prolonged rainy period.

Approach: *See* introductory notes for Windy Buttress.

Starting Point: As for Route 4.

Descent: Once at the summit of Windy Buttress, face inland and walk back and right into the thorn bushes where a small track will be found which leads to a scramble down the gully. Take care as the route can become very slippery and accidents have happened. Part way down the descent it is possible to traverse across to the Windy Ledge extension and Tiger Trot at a very exposed V. Diff.

Aurora was the first recorded route to be climbed at Stoney Middleton and the ascent was probably not repeated for twenty years. An early attempt by three young men resulted in one dead and two severely injured. Modern equipment and techniques ensure a better success rate.

The first pitch climbs a well-polished crack and groove to a ledge which leads left to an arête. Here a peg can be reached left of the arête on an adjacent route. The pitch continues up and right to a broken pillar which leads to a belay in the break level with Windy Ledge.

Moving right along the ledge into the trees brings one to the base of the second pitch, a clean, well-cracked corner. After the first 5m, progress can be made by well-balanced bridging and jamming. It is possible to follow the corner to its termination, but far finer to traverse out left some 5m below the top to a good ledge on the arête. From here, the starting point for the traverse Alcasan, there are superb views across Scoop Wall to Windhover. The last part of the route leads directly up the front of the arête to the flat, grassy summit. It is possible to take a belay just below the finish.

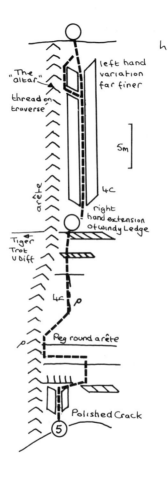

left hand
variation
far finer

"The "altar""

thread on
traverse

5m

arête

4C

right
hand extension
of windy Ledge

Tiger
Trot
V Diff

4c

Peg round arête

Polished Crack

5

6: MEMNON (E2) 51m

Summary: Two somewhat dis-connected pitches but both give good climbing and with some exciting situations on pitch 2.

First Ascent: The lower pitch – no recorded first ascent but it was almost certainly climbed as a mixed free and aid route in the early 1960s, the points of aid being sub-sequently wittled down by progressive generations of climbers. The upper pitch – Geoff Birtles and Chris Jackson in the spring of 1963, using 2 points of aid, and probably climbed free by the early 1970s.

Best Conditions: Both pitches dry quickly, the top pitch particularly so. Because of the easy access along Windy Ledge, many parties choose to climb the top pitch only.

Approach: *See* introductory notes for Windy Buttress.

Starting Point: Right of the toe of Windy Buttress. A few easy ledges lead up into an obvious huge corner above a flat ledge.

Descent: As for Route 5.

Two contrasting pitches, the first an enclosed corner system with good resting places, the second, bold face climbing, which will leave you with aching forearms. Both pitches contain a light sprinkling of old pegs and bits of tat. The crux of pitch 2, which consists of surmounting a bulge above the projecting ledge, is protected by a peg which has been driven too far in and may require threading. The direct finish at E3 5c is rarely done; most parties head for the comforts of the crack and corner on the right once they have reached the traverse line taken by Alcasan (4).

Bill Wintrip on Memnon (Route 6), Windy Buttress, Stoney Middleton. (Photo: Chris Jackson.)

7: SCOOP WALL (E2) 27m

Summary: Originally an aid route, Scoop Wall is now one of Stoney Middleton's finest climbs at this grade and takes the centre of the huge scooped face of Windy Buttress. The climbing is steep and strenuous, with the technical crux close to the top. The climb can be split at the shallow cave on the right at two-thirds height. Protection is excellent throughout and there is some *in situ* gear.

First Ascent: Roy Leeming et al. in 1955, and first climbed free by T. Proctor and G. Birtles in 1967.

Best Conditions: At almost any time. There is little or no seepage except after prolonged and heavy rain.

Approach: *See* introductory notes for Windy Buttress.

Starting Point: Follow Windy Ledge around the arête of Windhover to a comfortable widening. The route starts below an obvious sentry box, left of the overhangs, at 3m.

Descent: As for Route 5.

Sustained and absorbing climbing, giving an excellent introduction to the harder routes on Windy Buttress. The route starts with energetic moves into the sentry box where good protection can be arranged. Strenuous layback moves follow round the overhang to the right, past an *in situ* sling to good hand jams and more good protection. Above this point, the crack closes up and it is difficult to obtain a resting position for the next 3m. Many a climber has taken to the air at this point, owing to prolonged and often fruitless attempts to place marginal protection. At the break, it is possible to traverse right into a shallow cave to take a belay, although most parties opt for the safer option of climbing the route as one pitch.

Above the break, the wall steepens and further progress appears unlikely. Do not despair, protection is good and there are several surprisingly sharp holds which help to offset the steepness of the climbing. The object of the exercise is to gain the wide crack high on the left, which leads to the top. The secret is not to grab for it too soon but to climb up the shallow corner on its right by wide bridging until the base of the crack is below shoulder height. The lower part of the crack takes good wires and if you find yourself in an alarming position, reach across and swing into the crack where better holds lead to the top.

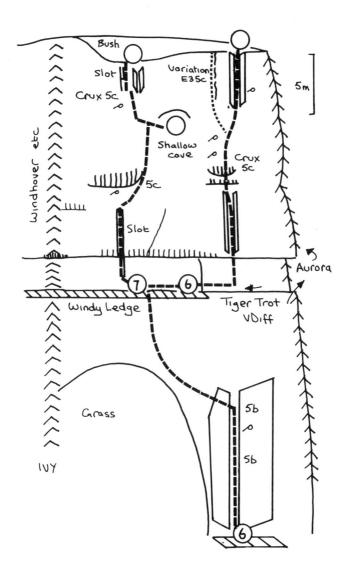

8: The Flakes (E2) 36m

Summary: Splendid climbing beneath the huge stepped overhang which runs across the front of Windy Buttress. The start, which is shared with Windhover and Armageddon is usually the crux, although this can change due to the transient nature of the rock at this point. An excellent variation finish can be taken that cuts through the left end of the overhangs, giving the route two superb pitches. There is some *in situ* protection and camming devices may be found useful beneath the overhangs.

First Ascent: R. Dearman and M. Battersby in 1964, as an aid route.

They declared that it would never be done 'free' but within a week this was reduced to one point of aid by Chris Jackson and Brian Starkey. The Flakes Direct was added later by G. Birtles.

Best Conditions: At any time, the route is rarely wet.

Approach: *See* introductory notes for Windy Buttress.

Starting Point: The route starts below the prominent square arete where Windy Ledge takes a left turn to the widening.

Descent: As for Route 5.

The first few moves up the overhanging and polished nose of the arête usually constitute the technical crux of the route. Several pieces of rock have broken away from the start over recent years and it is possible that the architecture will change yet again. Ensure that your second is well belayed – it is a long way to the deck.

Small wires protect the initial moves which require some determination, but once the face of the buttress is gained it is possible to stand in balance. The steep wall above is climbed past two peg runners to a thin flake and easier moves to the left lead under the overhangs. From this point onwards, the route is well-cracked and camming devices may be found useful. Traverse left for 5m, with an increasing sense of exposure, until it is possible to move up to beneath the final roof. A difficult move left brings you to an exposed and semi-hanging stance.

The normal finish is pleasant but something of an anticlimax, and takes the easy corner just beyond the belay. Far finer is the Flakes Direct, the variation finish. From the belay, move back right and make outrageous and difficult moves around the overhang into a shallow corner (shared by Armageddon). The difficulties are short-lived and well protected by a peg runner. Care should be taken that the foot does not slip on to the peg. Above, easier climbing leads over a final cracked overhang to the top. Belays are in the corner behind the block.

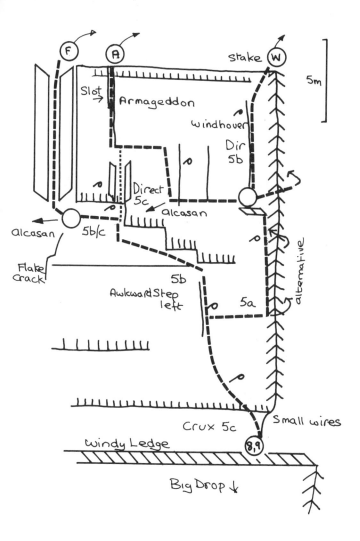

9: ARMAGEDDON & WINDHOVER DIRECT (E2, E2) 27m, 24m

Summary: These two routes share a common first pitch up the bold arête in the centre of Windy Buttress. For the second pitch, Armageddon takes a delectable traverse left above the overhangs of The Flakes, whereas Windhover Direct continues steeply up the arête following a thin crack line. A standard rack of gear plus a few extra clippers for the *in situ* pegs should protect either route.

First Ascent: Windhover – Dave Mellor and Dave Johnson in 1958, using several points of aid and more or less freed by Barry Webb in 1960. The Direct finish was added by Chris Jackson in 1963. Armageddon – Chris Jackson and Brian Starkey in 1964.

Best Conditions: At any time. It rarely stays wet but can be windy.

Approach: *See* introductory notes for Windy Buttress.

Starting Point: Below the prominent square arête where Windy Ledge takes a left turn to the widening.

Descent: As for Route 5.

The first pitch is common to both Armageddon and Windhover, and the first 10m is also shared with The Flakes (8). The difficult start, up the ever changing nose of the arête, leads to easier climbing. Occasionally a peg appears in this lower section but normally small wires are required for protection. Ensure that your second has a good belay.

Once established on the wall, it is possible to stand in balance and regain a little composure. The route climbs the wall, past two pegs, until a traverse right can be made to the arête. The arête is then followed using either side, as preferred, passing two more pegs to reach a superb stance on the left.

Armageddon traverses delicately left from the stance for 4m on perfect rock to a shallow corner. The position is exciting, particularly when you realize that the overhangs of The Flakes are just below your feet. From here, the route makes a rising traverse left to better holds and finishes up the prominent crack that splits a small overhang near the left edge of the buttress.

Windhover Direct takes the obvious thin crack behind the stance. The crack tapers from hand width to nothing in the next 4m and is more strenuous than initial appearances might suggest. However, it does lend itself to good protection. Above the crack, a good hold leads to easier climbing where it is possible to step right and finish up the edge of the buttress.

10

10: HOW THE HELL, WHAT THE HELL & MORNING CRACK (VS, VS, S), 26m

Summary: A set of three excellent climbs up prominent cracks on The Triglyph. The left hand crack, How The Hell, includes a classic off-width problem. The central crack, What The Hell, contains jamming and bridging in fine position. Protection is good on all; camming devices may be found useful, particularly on How The Hell.

First Ascent: How The Hell and Morning Crack – Joe Brown in 1950, What The Hell – Jack Soper, Neville Crowther and Dave Johnson in 1957. Gritstone training was brought to limestone problems.

Best Conditions: The routes dry rapidly even after prolonged rain.

Approach: *See* Approaches under Stoney Middleton. The Triglyph is a prominent, isolated buttress, high above the path, some 100m beyond The Promenade. A small track wanders up the hillside directly below the buttress.

Starting Point: What The Hell – at the lowest point of the buttress below a flat wall. How The Hell – to the left just right of the corner. Morning Crack – below the shorter right-hand crack.

Descent: Facing inland, walk back and right to the descent path.

How The Hell, an easy climb leads towards the left-hand crack which on closer acquaintance turns out to be a chimney. The climbing is perhaps best attempted facing right as the left wall cuts away rather sharply. It is tempting to plunge everything into the deep recesses of the crack, but holds on the walls provide a neater, though slightly bolder, solution to the problem. Above, climbing is less strenuous and the route finishes by traversing right below a large block.

For What The Hell, climb from the toe of the buttress towards the centre crack. The first part of the crack is best tackled by bridging and jamming, with an awkward move a little way below a widening. Here the route takes to a rib formed by the right side of the crack, using large and slightly suspect holds. Protection becomes difficult to arrange for the next metre or so although the climbing is not too demanding. Just below the top, the rock bulges and protection reappears in time for the final exposed moves onto the flat grassy finish.

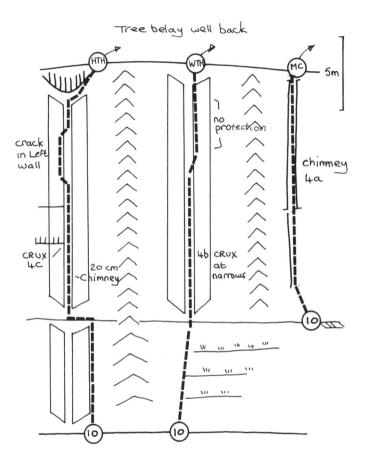

Tree belay well back

HTH

WTH

MC

5m

no protection

crack in Left wall

chimney 4a

CRUX 4C

20 cm Chimney

4b CRUX at narrows

10

10

10

Ravensdale

Ravensdale is a large west-facing buttress of natural limestone, high above, and opposite to, Ravensdale Cottages. Although the dale is commonly known as Ravensdale it is marked on the OS map as Cressbrook Dale. The crag is situated close to the rim of the valley and suffers little drainage so it can be climbed at most times of the year, but it can be exposed. Ravensdale has a number of high-quality medium grade routes which serve as an excellent introduction to climbing on limestone.

Approaches: It is possible to drive to Ravensdale Cottages where there is limited parking. From Sheffield, the T208 Trent bus calls at Tideswell, from where it is possible to walk to Ravensdale, via Litton village, in 30–40 minutes. From Manchester, the X67 bus also goes to Tideswell. From Bakewell, a bus goes to Monsal Head. From there, walk down into Monsal Dale and follow the road as far as Cressbrook Mill (currently a builder's yard). Climb the hill for 500m to a small road on the right signposted to Ravensdale. From Monsal Head to Ravensdale takes about 20 minutes. It is also possible to reach Ravensdale from Wardlow Mires (SK 181756) on the A623 or from Wardlow village (SK 182745) in about 15 and 20 minutes respectively.

   The approach to the foot of the crag is from the small car park by the cottages. The crag is situated in a nature reserve and **climbers are requested to use only this approach from the valley floor.** For the starting point for all the following routes, take the track from the car-park, steeply through the woods, to the toe of the main, Raven Buttress.

Accommodation: Camping – sites are thin on the ground in The Peak, the nearest regular one is probably at Hope, (SK 174833).
Bivouacs – inside a large draughty through cave at the left end of the crag.
Youth hostels – at Ravenstor (near Tideswell), Bakewell and Eyam.
Hotels, b. & b. – at Monsal Head and Upperdale Farm, as well as many other small hotels and pubs in the location.

Services: There are post offices at Tideswell, Litton and Great Longstone and telephones in Cressbrook village (up the hill), Litton, Wardlow and Wardlow Mires. Petrol stations can be found in Wardlow Mires, Tideswell and Great Longstone. There are pubs in all the villages, the nearest for those without transport is in Wardlow. Food can be obtained at Monsal Head (pub and café), at Upperdale Farm in Monsal Dale and in Tideswell, and there are shops in Litton and Tideswell. There are toilets in Tideswell and at the Tideswell Dale picnic spot 2km south on the B6049, also at Monsal Head.

A Concise History: Ravensdale was almost certainly explored as a climbing area well before the first recorded routes but, like many of these early visits, they were considered inconsequential, a mere diversion from the upland gritstone crags and, sadly, records were not kept. The first recorded routes appeared in November 1958 when John Loy, who was later to be author of many first ascents on Ravensdale, and Bill Woodward, discovered Frore. However, the most obvious lines, Medusa and Via Vita, were not climbed until Dave Johnson and Dave Mellor teamed up with John Loy and visited the crag in 1960. After that, development seems to have been sporadic until 1965/6 when many of the remaining big lines were climbed in preparation for the new climbing guide, Paul Nunn's *Northern Limestone*, which appeared in 1969. Clive and Ted Rowland were very active on the crag during this period, as were Alan Clarke, Rod Brown and Paul Nunn, and classics such as Conclusor, Mephistopheles and Via Vita Direct were added to the records. Over the next ten years, most of the aid points were eliminated from the routes. Apart from the addition of a handful of eliminate lines the crag stood much as it does today, albeit, a little less polished.

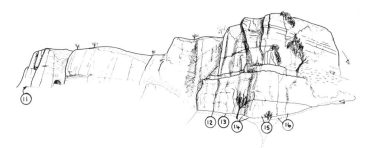

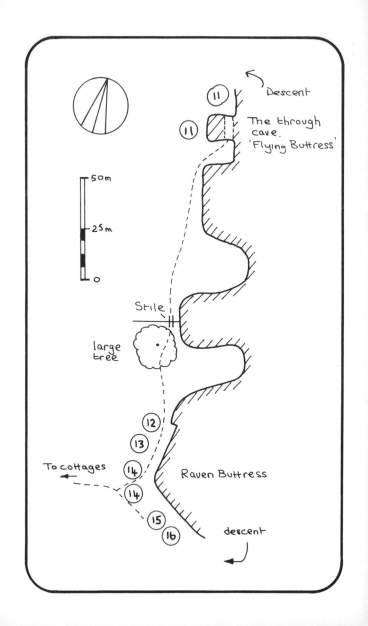

John Hall on Great Cleft (Route 50), Wildcat Crags, Matlock.
(Photo: Chris Jackson.)

11: GYMNIC, AMAIN & IMPENDENT (VS, VS, VS) 21m

Summary: Three popular routes close to the through cave of Flying Buttress at the left end of the crag. Gymnic is becoming very polished but still a worthwhile route. Amain has a strenuous start leading to a fine finishing corner. Impendent has fine jamming up a crack on the outside of the cave arch. Protection is generally good on all three routes.

First Ascent: Gymnic – John Loy, Harry Gillot, Brian Stokes and Ted Howard in 1960. Amain – John Loy, Dave Johnson and Dave Mellor in 1960. Impendent – John Loy and Dave Mellor in 1960.

Best Conditions: All dry quickly. Amain tends to be most sheltered.

Approach: *See* Approaches under Ravensdale. From the toe of the main, Raven Buttress, follow the track, bearing left, for 150m to the through cave of Flying Buttress.

Starting Points: Gymnic – at thin cracks just left of the cave. Amain – at an overhanging crack at the right-hand side of the cave entrance, opposite Gymnic. Impendent – on the outside face of the through cave.

Descent: Walk up the hillside then follow a path, bearing left, to an easy descent gully.

These three routes form a popular set for most visiting parties. Gymnic starts off as a polished face climb up thin cracks to a small overhang. It is delightful climbing but the polish instils a certain lack of confidence in the feet with the resulting aching forearms. The overhang is easier than it looks, and the corner above is just good fun. Finish either to the left or right of it.

Amain pulls no punches for the first few moves. A vicious, overhanging start soon relents however, to a good resting ledge where it is possible to regain a little composure. Above, follow the corner or take the hanging flake on the left wall, in fine position, as an alternative finish.

Impendent will cause no problems to those who have cut their teeth on gritstone cracks. Fine jamming but with a big prickly drop below.

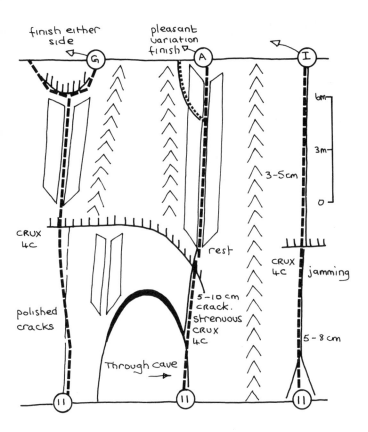

finish either side

pleasant variation finish

G

A

I

6m

3m

3-5cm

0

CRUX 4C

rest

CRUX 4C

jamming

polished cracks

5-10 cm CRACK. strenuous CRUX 4C

5-8 cm

Through cave →

12: CONCLUSOR (HVS) 46m

Summary: A good climb with a splendid upper pitch, steep and in superb position, with a thought-provoking crux. Protection is excellent throughout.

First Ascent: A much tried line, finally falling to Clive Rowland and Paul Nunn in 1964.

Best Conditions: The route follows a crack line which may hold some dampness after a wet spell.

Approach: *See* Approaches under Ravensdale.

Starting Point: Below a clean corner at the left end of Raven Buttress, just right of a prominent crack.

Descent: From the summit of the buttress, facing inland, walk back and right to a track leading down the descent gully.

Conclusor is one of those routes which is better than it looks and what appears to be a rather scruffy section of crag conceals some fine climbing. The first pitch is straightforward and leads you to a small ledge with an ivy-covered block for company. Above, the rock steepens and the groove, which is the main feature of the upper pitch, can be seen.

On an early attempt by Clive and Ted Rowland a huge block detached itself from the face along with Ted, cutting a swathe through the trees, and almost reaching the cottages. So great was the trundle that it featured in the *Derbyshire Times* the following week. The climbers survived to tell the tale despite the belay being partly cut by the falling block.

The first moves of the second pitch are steep but they can be avoided by climbing up on the left and stepping into the groove higher up. Absorbing climbing past an ancient peg leads to the crux, a long pull through from a perfect finger jam to good holds. The finger jam also takes a perfect nut but if you choose one which is too large you will not get your fingers into it. The final section is easier but still in fine position and takes a wider crack behind a series of flakes, past a good ledge to the top, where there is a block belay.

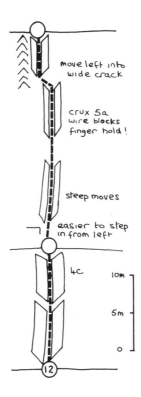

move left into
wide crack

crux 5a
wire blocks
finger hold !

steep moves

easier to step
in from left

4c

10m

5m

0

12

13: MEDUSA & VIA VITA (VS, HVS)
46m, 49m

Summary: Two of the Peak's trade routes. Enjoyable climbs with a 'big wall' feel about them, set amongst some impressive rock architecture. Protection is good.

First Ascent: Medusa – Dave Johnson and Dave Mellor in 1960. Via Vita – John Loy and Dave Mellor in 1960. Direct free – possibly Chris Jackson in 1976.

Best Conditions: The routes dry fairly rapidly although the final corner of Medusa may retain some dampness.

Approach: *See* Approaches under Ravensdale.

Starting Point: Left of the toe of the buttress is a large tree, start at a very polished flake crack some 6m to the left of it.

Descent: From the summit of the buttress, facing inland, walk back and right to a track leading down the descent gully.

Medusa is probably Ravensdale's most popular route, a fine expedition at its grade. The polished start leads up a flake crack which curves over to form a spike which will accommodate a long sling. Above, a short but steep wall leads to a good ledge with a peg. Medusa now traverses right to a belay in the corner system which forms the left side of a great prow of rock. The rest of the climb follows the corner system, using the pleasant, slabby left wall most of the way until things narrow down and the bulging right wall pushes you around a rib into the easier finishing groove.

Via Vita starts in the same way as Medusa up to the ledge and although it is possible to belay here it is better to continue up the crack to the next belay. Above, the hand traverse to the hanging ledge, which brings one to the crux, is technically easy but ridiculously exposed. Legend has it that it was originally climbed in boots with a peg, three falls and half a packet of fags for aid, which seems reasonable. The bulging wall is climbed by a widening crack on the right next to a huge overhanging fin of limestone. Entry to the crack is awkward and in an incredible position but, once gained, the climbing rapidly eases and the top arrives too soon. There are sledge iron belays in the grass close to the edge.

For those who require a little extra from the route, it is possible to climb the prominent overhanging V-groove which runs down from the fin to the belay at the top of pitch 2. Entry is difficult but good protection can be arranged prior to commitment. Once ensconced, there are better holds and easier climbing leads up to the 'ordinary' route.

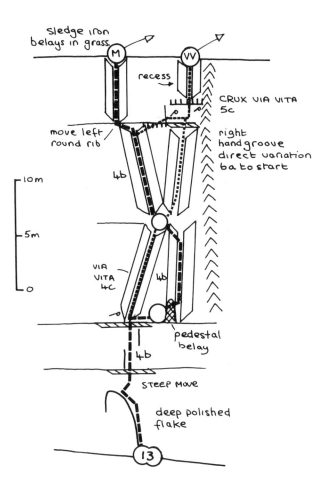

sledge iron
belays in grass

M

VV

recess

CRUX VIA VITA
5c

move left
round rib

right
hand groove
direct variation
6a to start

10m

5m

4b

0

VIA
VITA
4C

4b

pedestal
belay

4b

STEEP MOVE

deep polished
flake

13

14: MEALY BUGS & MEALYSTOPHELES (VS, VS) 46m

Summary: Two steep and pleasant crack lines with a fine mountaineering atmosphere. The starts are becoming somewhat polished and may be found to be good value at the grade. Protection is generally adequate.

First Ascents: Mealy Bugs – Dave Johnson and Dave Mellor in May 1960. Mealystopheles – Bob Dearman and Rod Brown in April 1965. Only the first pitch was climbed as new; the top pitch had been previously climbed by Johnson and Mellor as a variation finish to Mealy Bugs.

Best Conditions: Both routes dry fairly quickly, although the lower crack of Mealy Bugs can retain some dampness after a wet spell.

Approach: *See* Approaches under Ravensdale.

Starting Point: Left of the toe of the buttress is a prominent tree. Mealy Bugs starts below the obvious chimney/crack line just right of it. Mealystopheles also starts below the shallow chimney and to the right, just left of the toe of the buttress.

Descent: From the summit of the buttress, facing inland, walk back and right to a track leading down the descent gully.

The chimney crack at the start of Mealy Bugs is actually harder than it looks, and the widening at about 10m provides an awkward move a little way above your runners. It is easiest to face left and to step out left to a small square toe hold, which is not readily visible until one is committed to the move. Above, things assume normality to the stance. The second pitch, though technically easier than the first, is perhaps psychologically no less demanding. The traverse across the scooped wall is not well protected and some larger nuts or camming devices might be found useful in the final crack, which finishes in superb position.

Mealystopheles gives a fine, sustained start with good protection round the strenuous little roof at around 8m and shares a stance with Mealy Bugs. Above, the upper corner of Mealy Bugs is followed to an intimidating little traverse to the right, around the arête into the wide finishing crack of Mephistopheles. There is an ancient peg on the traverse into the chimney but this is not to be trusted.

Dave Edwards on Easter Island (Route 66), Ilam Rock, Dovedale.
(Photo: Chris Jackson.)

15: MEPHISTOPHELES & PURPLE HAZE (HVS, HVS) 45m, 45m

Summary: Two enjoyable companion routes offering steep but well-protected climbing.

First Ascent: Mephistopheles – Paul Nunn and Oliver Woolcock in 1964, with 1 point of aid on pitch 2. Purple Haze – Bob Dearman and Dave Riley in June 1970, using 2 points of aid, and subsequently freed by Keith Myhill and Tom Proctor on the second ascent.

Best Conditions: At almost any time as there is very little drainage but the routes can be somewhat exposed to the wind.

Approach: *See* Approaches under Ravensdale.

Starting Point: Mephistopheles – below a wedged block, just right of the toe of the buttress and left of a prickly bush. Purple Haze – below a thin flake behind the prickly bush.

Descent: From the summit of the buttress, facing inland, walk back and right to a track leading down the descent gully.

The first pitch of Mephistopheles follows the broad front of the buttress, giving pleasant and varied climbing. The start takes a steep, slabby wall to a large perched block where the route steepens. Starting the bulge is awkward, although the proximity of an old peg runner definitely helps. Jugs soon come to hand and the going eases as you approach a good ledge. Nunn and Woolcock originally used a point of aid on pitch 2 but since then bits have dropped off, new holds have appeared and wired nuts have been invented. The climbing is steep and strenuous for a couple of moves but is very protectable. A crank up on a locking finger jam, just over the bulge, allows a high foot-ledge to be gained. From here the wide finishing cracks are almost within reach.

Purple Haze enjoys its crux in the early sections of the route and the moves from the thin flake into the groove above can be found quite strenuous. The second pitch, though technically easier than the first, finishes in fine position up the unlikely-looking upper wall.

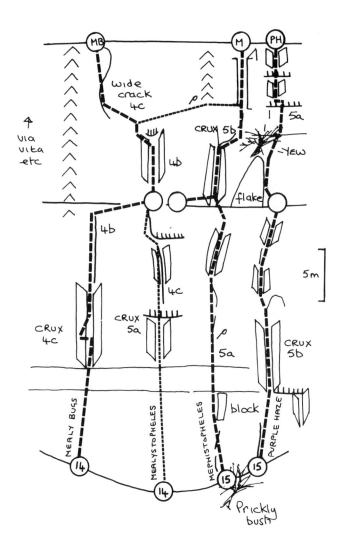

16: FRORE & PLOY (VS, VS)
43m, 50m

Summary: Two worthwhile outings with some good positions,
unfortunately broken by a grassy
terrace between pitches.

First Ascents: Frore – John Loy
and Bill Woodward in 1958. It was
almost certainly a rediscovery of
Flypaper which was the first, but
vaguely recorded, route at Ravensdale. Ploy – Oliver Woolcock
and Rod Brown in June 1964.

Best Conditions: Neither route is
particularly prone to seepage and
both dry fairly quickly.

Approach: *See* Approaches under
Ravensdale.

Starting Points: Ploy – below an
overhung corner, right of the Haw-
thorn bush, which is to the right of
the toe of the buttress. Frore – at
the shallow groove 2m to the right
of Ploy.

Descent: From the summit of the
buttress, facing inland, walk back
and right to a track leading down
the descent gully.

Despite the broad band of grass splitting the buttress at this point, and
the obvious escapability, both routes are well worth while. Frore probably
contains the hardest moves on the two routes; the little scooped corner
requires a slight degree of athleticism to reach a strange 'cemented' jug,
from where it is possible to move right to easier ground. The upper pitches
of both routes share a couple of metres of the corner which flanks the
right side of the fine upper wall. Here, Ploy has the most exposed climbing
but with the dubious comforts of an ancient peg.

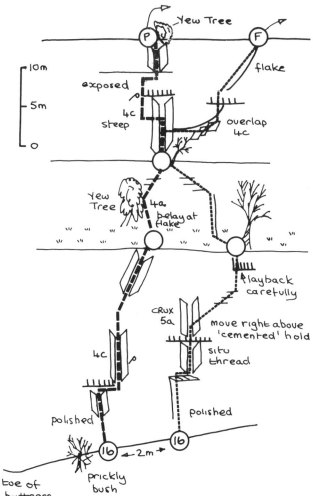

Chee Dale Area

The River Wye runs east from Buxton, passing through Bakewell to join the River Derwent at Rowsley near Matlock. On its way, the river cuts through a series of deep and beautiful valleys, which contain the highest concentration of limestone climbing in The Peak. One of these is Chee Dale.

At the west end of the valley, Chee Dale is wide and grassy, but it becomes progressively more gorge like as one travels east towards Chee Tor. In summer, the fertile valley floor around Chee Tor sports much exotic flora including giant butterburs, reminiscent of rhubarb but over 2m high, giving some sections a lost world atmosphere. Currently, the area is a forcing ground for some of the hardest routes in Britain but as well as the modern super routes there is also a wealth of splendid classic climbs of a less demanding nature; it is indeed a dale for all climbers.

An abandoned railway line cuts through the dale giving convenient access to some of the buttresses. Unfortunately, the longest tunnel has been closed off.

Two kilometres east of Chee Tor, the valley is crossed by a huge railway viaduct and the B6049 Tideswell road. Beyond this, the river flows through Miller's Dale and Water-cum-Jolly before reaching the gentler-shaped Monsal Dale. Water-cum-Jolly is the old name for the lower end of Miller's Dale and only features on the OS maps revised in 1986. However, the name is used by climbers to describe the stretch of valley between Litton and Cressbrook mills.

The quality of the rock varies along the length of the valley but much of it is perfect water-worn limestone, often with solution pockets. The narrow section of valley containing Chee Tor is surrounded by jungle and is prone to seepage, so that for much of the winter, and after prolonged wet spells, climbing is not possible. Plum Buttress at the west end of the valley tends to dry more quickly.

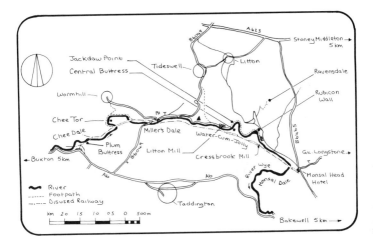

Stoney Middleton 5 km

Jackdaw Point
Central Buttress
Tideswell
Litton

Ravensdale
Rubicon Wall

Wormhill

Chee Tor
Chee Dale
Plum Buttress

Miller's Dale

Water-cum-Jolly
Litton Mill
Cressbrook Mill

Gt. Longstone

Buxton 5 km

A6

Taddington

River Wye
Monsal Dale

Monsal Head Hotel

Bakewell 5 km

River
Footpath
Disused Railway

km   2.0   1.5   1.0   0.5   0   500m

PLUM BUTTRESS

Plum Buttress faces north and is situated at the western end of Chee Dale on the true right bank of the river. It is best viewed from the disused railway line (The Monsal Trail) and is difficult to miss as the huge overhanging upper section dominates this section of the valley. If exposure brings on your dizzy spells, this is not the crag for you as the climbing on the upper walls crosses some audacious territory.

Approaches: The closest approach to the west end of Chee Dale is from the A6 Buxton to Bakewell road. The T208 bus service from Sheffield to Buxton and Hanley stops at Topley Pike and there is a service between Buxton and Bakewell. There is also a rail service to Buxton from Manchester.

For those with transport the best approach is from the car-park on the A6 at SK 112726. This is situated at a bend in the road giving views down to a small group of cottages and the Great Rocks Dale quarries beyond. A small path wanders down the steep grassy hillside to a footbridge spanning the disused railway. Cross the stile on the left and follow the railway rightward for 400m.

It is possible to approach Plum Buttress from Topley Pike (SK 104725) where a track leads downstream to cottages. **Do not park at the cottages or obstruct the track in any way.** From the end of the track follow a path onto the disused railway. Plum Buttress may also be approached by the scenic route from Miller's Dale station (car-park) or from Wormhill (*See* Approaches for Chee Tor).

Accommodation: Camping – the valley is a nature reserve and camping is not allowed. There is a campsite in Buxton.
Youth hostels – at Buxton and Ravenstor.
Bivouacs – it would be possible to bivouac in the disused railway tunnels. Some of the overhanging buttresses may give shelter outside the rainy season. Please take your litter home.
Hotels, b. & b. – numerous in Buxton.

Services: A good selection of most things can be found in Buxton, 5km from Topley Pike.

17: SIRPLUM (E1) 60m

Summary: A tremendous route, taking the steep lower wall and hanging ramp line into the overhangs above the huge nose of Plum Buttress. Pitch 2 is well protected but strenuous and in a very exposed position. In the event of a fall from the end of the ramp which involves loss of contact with the rock, there may be insufficient rope to lower the climber to the ground. The carrying of some thin line that could be used for prusiking is recommended.

First Ascent: Bob Dearman and Rod Brown in 1964. Some aid was used, which has been eliminated by subsequent ascents.

Best Conditions: The crag faces north and can be cold and draughty in the winter months, although its open position allows it to dry relatively quickly after a wet spell.

Approach: *See* Approaches under Plum Buttress. From the disused railway track, descend the embankment and cross the hillside to the foot of the crag.

Starting Point: Start a few metres right of the widest point of the overhang, a grassy start leads to a slight corner.

Descent: From the grass bank at the top of the route, carefully traverse left facing inland until the descent gully is reached.

Sirplum has an audacious second pitch. The most technical move is at the start of pitch 2 but this is rarely regarded as the crux as the overhanging juggy section below the final groove usually causes most problems. Prior to this, close to the nose of the buttress is a large natural thread which will require a double length sling; this is no place to be joining slings together. Beyond the thread, it is possible to traverse low, but easier to move up and round a rib to a concealed peg below the final groove. Above, things ease a little but a combination of tired arms and steep rock demand some determination from the climber. The occasional suspect block in the final groove should be treated with respect.

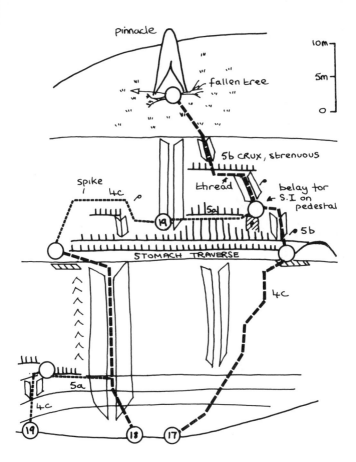

18: THE STALK (VS) 27m

Summary: The easiest route on the buttress. Enjoyable climbing up the prominent right-facing corner at the left side of the buttress. The climb mainly follows the right wall of the corner and finishes with strenuous or undignified moves on to the belay ledge.

First Ascent: Harold Drasdo and Gordon Mansell in 1955. It was probably the first significant route to be climbed in Chee Dale.

Best Conditions: The route dries fairly quickly after rain although, since it faces north, the route may hold damp patches for much of the winter.

Approach: *See* Approaches under Plum Buttress. From the disused railway track, descend the embankment and cross the hillside to the foot of the crag.

Starting Point: Just right of the obvious corner.

Descent: Traverse left into the prominent grassy gully.

A pleasant and popular climb giving excellent views across to the modern horrors on the main overhangs. The upper reaches of the corner are well cracked and will take some good protection. Belay to an array of perched blocks above the pitch; attachment to more than one of these is recommended.

19: THE SUPER INDIRECT (E1) 120m

Summary: A superb *tour de force*, combining the four routes – Sarin, The Stalk, Aplomb and pitch 2 of Sirplum – to give a climb of unforgettable exposure. One of the best outings at this grade in The Peak but it is not for the timid. Protection is generally good but can be a little difficult to arrange on pitch 4.

First Ascent: Pitches 1 and 2 (which is Sarin) – Paul Nunn and Trevor Briggs in 1966. Pitch 3 is part of The Stalk (18). Pitch 4 (which is Aplomb) – Jeff Morgan and Bob Toogood in 1968. Pitch 5 is the top pitch of Sirplum (17).

Best Conditions: It can be cold and draughty in the winter months. Pitch 4 may hold some dampness, otherwise the route dries fairly quickly.

Approach: *See* Approaches under Plum Buttress. From the disused railway track, descend the embankment and cross the hillside to the foot of the crag.

Starting Point: Start some 20m left of the corner of The Stalk (18) at a ledge some 3m above the grass bank.

Descent: Traverse left into the prominent grassy gully.

The excitement starts on pitch 2. The traverse into The Stalk is somewhat steeper than appearances from the ground might suggest. Once established in The Stalk, it is usually found necessary to take a belay after a few metres to avoid excessive rope drag, although good ropework might allow the ledge at the top of the corner to be reached. The start of pitch 4 is a little scrappy, but once the spike is reached things rapidly improve and a descending line takes one to a hanging stance on the lip of the roofs of The Big Plum. The next pitch is very exposed and traverses the break across the nose of the buttress. There is normally adequate *in situ* gear in the traverse to allow Sirplum to be reached without dalliance; indeed a bolt has appeared as part of a new route crossing the traverse. The break is very irregular and the fixing of further protection may be found to be a tiring proposition. The route joins Sirplum at a detached pedestal (take care at this point) with good belay wires possible in the crack above, and finishes with Sirplum (17) – a fitting climax to the route.

CHEE TOR

Chee Tor, 400m long and 50m high, is one of The Peak's finest crags and contains a wealth of classic climbs. Set in dramatic surroundings, the crag lines the true right bank of the River Wye, from the stepping stones just below the disused railway bridge where the dale becomes a gorge, and continues to where the path climbs above the river near the junction with Flag Dale and Wormhill Springs. Chee Tor is screened by trees, and unfortunately can become very damp and slimy in wet weather, so for most of the winter months it may be out of condition.

For the first time visitor, Chee Tor can be a confusing crag due to its lack of major features. The main feature visible from across the river is the open corner taken by Alfresco, towards the downstream, left end of the crag. On closer inspection, approximately half way along the crag there is a small slab of rock leaning against the foot of an overhanging wall. This is referred to in the descriptions and shown on the plan of Chee Tor.

Approaches: For those with transport, Chee Tor can be approached from the village of Wormhill or from the disused Miller's Dale station and then following the disused railway and valley floor to Wormhill Springs and then Chee Tor.

For those without wheels, the T208 bus service from Sheffield to Hanley stops at Miller's Dale. The disused railway station can be found by taking the minor road off the main B6049, on the Buxton side of the railway bridge. There is a small café opposite the station.

From Wormhill, follow the track that runs south from the dip in the road at SK 124739, which leads by various routes to the valley floor near a prominent resurgence or by Wormhill Springs. Walking in the upstream direction, the path climbs then drops down rocky steps into the narrow downstream end of Chee Tor. It will take you 10 minutes down from Wormhill and 20 minutes going back as it is uphill.

From the car-park at Miller's Dale station (SK 138732), follow the disused railway track westwards until directed down to the riverside path at a very high bridge. Follow the path upstream, past Wormhill Springs and Flag Dale and into the gorge as before. This takes twenty minutes.

Accommodation: Camping – the valley is a nature reserve and camping is not allowed. There are campsites at Buxton and at Blackwell (SK 125721). Youth hostels – at Buxton and Ravenstor.

Bivouacs – various overhanging buttresses upstream of Chee Tor may provide shelter, although there is nothing outstanding. Remember that the valley is a nature reserve. Please respect nature and **take your litter home**.

B. & b. – there are numerous places in Buxton and Tideswell.

Services: There is a good selection of shops, a post office, a bank, a garage and numerous pubs in Tideswell, and small, somewhat seasonal, cafés in Wormhill and opposite Miller's Dale station. There are telephones at Wormhill, Miller's Dale (near The Angler's Rest) and in Tideswell. There are no pubs in Wormhill, the closest is The Angler's Rest.

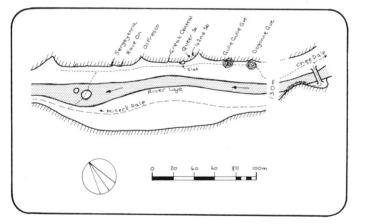

20: QUEER STREET, 42ND STREET & SUNNY GOODGE STREET (E3, E3, E2) 25m, 23m, 25m

Summary: Three superb, steep routes on near perfect rock, epitomizing the climbing on Chee Tor. Queer Street, which is steep and fingery, takes the left-hand crack; 42nd Street, less strenuous but bold at the crux, takes the central crack and Sunny Goodge Street, with a protected but intimidating traverse, takes the right-hand flake crack.

First Ascents: Queer Street and 42nd Street – Tom Proctor and Chris Jackson in August 1971. Sunny Goodge Street – Al Evans and friends in 1977.

Best Conditions: Chee Tor is screened by trees and vegetation and as such is slow to dry after a prolonged wet spell. The best conditions are usually found in spring and early summer when this west-facing crag can receive a good deal of afternoon sunshine. In winter, the deepness of the gorge prevents any sun from reaching the rock and it can remain damp and slimy for long periods.

Approach: *See* Approaches under Chee Tor. The approach is from Wormhill or Miller's Dale station. From the gorge at the downstream end of Chee Tor, those with no fear of alligators can paddle or boulder hop via Rhubarb Island (floods permitting). This gives access to the left-hand end of the crag. Otherwise, walk upstream, cross the footbridge and follow the true right bank for several hundred metres until rock appears.

Starting Point: Queer Street – a few metres right of the small leaning slab of rock, on sloping ground below a thin finger crack. 42nd Street – a few metres to the right of Queer Street. Sunny Goodge Street – a few metres to the right of 42nd Street.

Descent: Traverse right along the break until a suitable abseil point can be found.

Queer Street and 42nd Street are two Proctor classics. Queer Street is technically the harder of the two routes but excellent protection can be arranged and aspiring desperadoes often clock up flying hours on the crux. Above the crux, it is possible to gain a rest, which is worth taking as the rest of the route still contains some steep, bold moves.

42nd Street will suit those with a little less imagination. The climbing is well protected up to the rightward-curving ramp-line, but above this the crux arrives in the form of a couple of bold and committing moves onto the upper wall. A long reach, however, can be an advantage in placing protection on the crux.

Sunny Goodge Street is often a route of much deliberation. The disappearing corner becomes steeper prior to disappearing but takes some good wires. The next section constitutes the crux and on first acquaintance can be a little daunting. It is necessary to make a couple of strenuous, probably irreversible, moves out right to hidden but excellent holds in the ledge below the obvious flake crack. Once there, it is possible to regain a little composure, assure your second that there was really nothing to it, and to place yet another runner in the superb flake crack above. Good relations may well depend on a little consideration in the rope work.

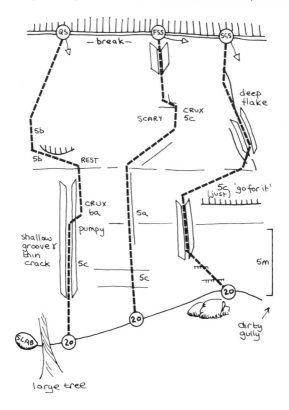

21: GREAT CENTRAL ROUTE (E1) 45m

Summary: The classic of the crag, with an upper pitch that finishes in grand position. Groove and wall climbing lead to a trying bulge which guards the upper pitch and constitutes the crux.

First Ascent: Rod Brown and Alan Wright in the winter of 1963, using a lot of aid. This was whittled down to a few points of aid by Joe Brown and John Cheesmond during the better weather of 1964, and by 1970 it was down to 2 points, which were probably used to gain the upper pitch. The first free ascent is not recorded.

Best Conditions: Dries slowly after a wet spell. Late spring or early summer is probably the most reliable time. *See* Best Conditions for Route 20.

Approach: *See* Approaches under Chee Tor.

Starting Point: Some 15m left of the small leaning slab of rock, below a shallow groove which is below and left of the prominent groove above the break.

Descent: Fight your way through primeval forest, bearing right, to find a suitable fat abseil tree. A double 45m rope will just reach the ground if you have picked the correct tree; make sure that you have!

A splendid route, although becoming a little polished, taking one of the easiest and best lines to the top of the crag. The climbing is extremely varied and always in good position. Above the sapling, the move out right into the flake below the belay on pitch one can be perplexing on first acquaintance but not too difficult once committed. Protection is excellent but some skill with rope work is required to make the most of it. Do not be tempted to climb the corner instead of the flake; it is much harder and the scene of many a flyer.

The entry into the flake crack on pitch 2 constitutes the crux of the route but is usually well protected by tat hanging down from an ancient peg. Using a point of aid here probably reduces the overall grade of the route to HVS. Above this some larger nuts or camming devices may be found useful. Keep your cool, there are good holds as well as tremendous position.

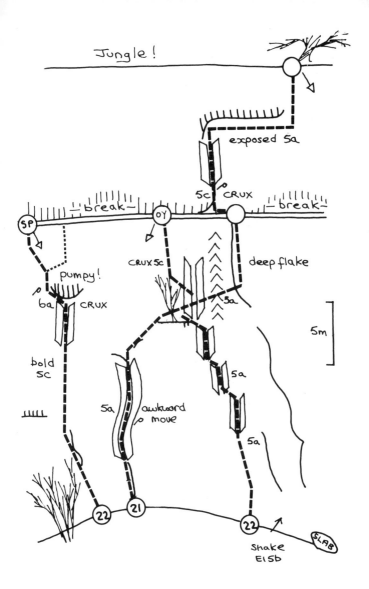

22: SPLINTERED PERSPEX & OF YOUTH (E3, E2) 23m, 23m

Summary: Companion routes, steep and continuously interesting. Splintered Perspex is considerably more strenuous than Of Youth and should be considered to be towards the top of its grade.

First Ascents: John Fleming and friends in July 1981. Famous for his 'air time', legend has it that Fleming totalled some 100m of falls on Splintered Perspex, ultimately having to rest on the peg to avoid clocking up some more. Subsequent ascents soon eliminated the rest point, after the optimum line for the next series of moves became established.

Best Conditions: *See* Best Conditions for Route 20.

Approach: *See* Approaches under Chee Tor.

Starting Point: Of Youth – at a sapling some 4m right of Great Central Route (21). This is a few metres left of a flake crack which starts at 4m and is taken by the route Shake (E1 5b). Splintered Perspex – just left of Great Central Route and below a small groove at mid-height.

Descent: Traverse the break to find a suitable thread for abseil.

Of Youth is often the scene of much confusion and interweaving of ropes as it crosses Great Central Route at the sapling. The crux arrives above the sapling, best tackled by moving right after initial moves, then back into the centre of the wall in tiring position. Above, a couple of reachy moves allows easier climbing and the break to be reached.

Splintered Perspex contains some steep and strenuous climbing, with committing moves around the bulge. A peg runner gives added confidence but those who dally here will probably find themselves dangling from it. Above, things are only slightly less steep and there are a variety of options, most are possible but moving slightly left and then up is probably the least difficult.

23: APPROACHING (E3) 23m

Summary: Steep, technical climbing, with an intimidating crux which proves to be a little easier than it looks. Protection is somewhat spaced around the mid-point where a confident approach should pay dividends.

First Ascent: Gary Gibson and A. Hudson in September 1983.

Best Conditions: *See* Best Conditions for Route 20.

Approach: *See* Approaches under Chee Tor.

Starting Point: Left of Great Central (21) is a prominent white groove below the upper break, taken by the splendid Ceramic (E4 6a). Approaching starts some 2m left of this.

Descent: By abseil, usually from a bunch of tat in the break.

This is the kind of route which once you have done it seems low in its grade but from below the crux, it can appear quite daunting. Good runners are left below a balancy white scoop and it is necessary to make several moves, out right, up, then back to the left below a bulge, without sign of more protection. In fact it is possible to arrange some on the traverse left. One more awkward step gains a groove and runners with deceptively reasonable moves, which lead to the final moves of Meditation and up to the break. Looking back, the moves seem to have been barely 5c but then memory is short and hindsight is a wonderful thing.

24: MEDITATION &
VALENTINE/ALFRESCO (E1, E1)
27m, 27m

Summary: Enjoyable climbing on superb pocketed rock. Valentine has been combined with the top pitch of Alfresco (HVS 5b) to give a balanced two-pitch route to the top of the crag but is commonly terminated at the break, giving a HVS. Both routes can be well protected by natural threads and small to medium wires.

First Ascents: Valentine – Jeff Morgan and H. Mares on 14 February 1970. A nut for aid was used on pitch 1. Meditation – Jim Moran and G. Traish in August 1977. Alfresco – J. Taylor and Graham West in 1960 as a partial aid route.

Best Conditions: The upper corner of Alfresco dries slowly after a wet spell and the break can be wet at this point. Late spring to early summer is probably the most reliable time. There are no special problems when finishing at the break. *See* Best Conditions for Route 20.

Approach: *See* Approaches under Chee Tor. Once you have reached the right-hand end of the crag, continue left for 100m along the foot of the crag towards the large open corner taken by Alfresco, the largest single feature on the crag.

Starting Points: Valentine – 11m right of the corner of Alfresco and left of Approaching, below two saplings on a line which trends left. Meditation – at a shallow groove 6m right of the corner, with a sapling at 3m.

Descent: Meditation – abseil from *in situ* threads in the break. Valentine/Alfresco – abseil from any suitable tree.

These two routes take opposing lines up the crag, crossing at mid-height. Meditation is one of Chee Tor's most popular routes and as such is gaining a little polish in places. There are a couple of awkward moves on the traverse, protected by a natural thread, but the crux comes as an exhilarating sting in the tail only a metre or so from the break. The counter line, Valentine, is a little easier to the break and many parties choose to finish here and abseil off. For the true mountain men, the traverse into the corner and the moves round the overhang will provide the highlights: steep, sometimes damp, a little shaky and with jungle to greet you.

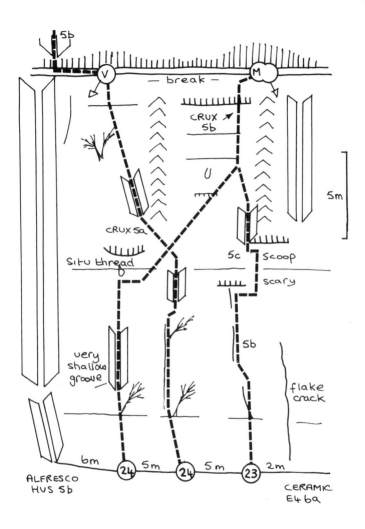

5b

V — break — M

CRUX ↗
5b

U

5m

CRUX 5a

Situ thread

5c   Scoop

scary

5b

very
shallow
groove

flake
crack

6m   ⑤24   5m   ⑤24   5m   ㉓23   2m

ALFRESCO
HVS 5b

CERAMIC
E4 6a

25: NOSTRADAMUS & RAVE ON (E1, E3) 25m, 25m

Summary: A common start serves these two routes but beyond that there is little similarity Nostradamus contains some elegant climbing between rest points whereas Rave On is steep and uncompromising with a problematical move to reach the jamming crack. Both routes contain some excellent climbing and can be adequately protected.

First Ascents: Nostradamus – Jeff Morgan and Dave Lester in April 1970 using 2 points of aid. The first free ascent is not recorded. Rave On – Geoff Birtles, Ernie Marshall and Al Evans in 1976.

Best Conditions: *See* Best Conditions for Route 20.

Approach: Continue left past the corner of Alfresco, passing below the leaning wall taken by Fawcett's Tequila Mockingbird (E6 6b) to a thin groove which starts at 4m and has a prominent flake to its right.

Starting Point: Both routes start below the thin left-facing groove taken by Nostradamus.

Descent: Traverse left and abseil from a suitable tree.

Originally graded E2, Rave On came as a bit of a shock to quite a few parties. The start is common with Nostradamus and most climbers clip the peg runner on that route before moving into steeper territory on the right. The crux is reaching the broad jamming crack above the flake and, once there, continuing on sagging arms. The crack takes some good gear but desperate attempts to fix this with tiring fingers have sometimes been followed by aerobatic displays. Nostradamus is altogether a more civilized affair after the initial steep moves, although she saves an awkward move for the finish at the break. Belay in the large tree in the corner.

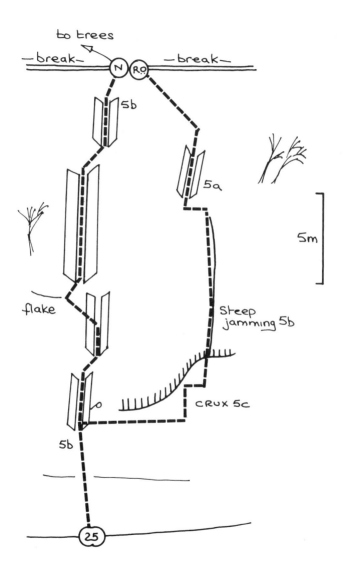

26: HERGIANI & SERGEYENNA (E2, E1) 45m, 30m

Summary: The classic pair for this part of the crag. Both routes can be adequately protected by natural threads and small-to-medium wires. Camming devices may be found useful at the roof on Sergeyenna.

First Ascents: Hergiani – Paul Nunn and Oliver Woolcock as HVS and A1 in 1965, and free by the early 1970s. Sergeyenna – Bob Dearman and D. Gill in 1966 as an aid route, and climbed free by Jerry Peel, Chris Gibb and Steve Foster in 1976.

Best Conditions: Sergeyenna dries slowly after a wet spell as water weeps from the roof. Late spring to early summer is probably the most reliable time. *See* Best Conditions for Route 20.

Approach: *See* Approaches under Chee Tor. Towards the left end of the crag, left of the groove of Nostradamus, is an obvious dark-coloured slab known as Nameless Wall. It can be recognized by the frieze of overhangs along its top and an undercut base. This part of the crag is usually approached by island hopping across the river, unless it is in flood.

Starting Points: Hergiani – at the right end of the lower wall of the slab, at a prominent flake crack leading to a small ledge. Sergeyenna – some 6m left at a thin crack in the steep lower wall.

Descent: By abseil from a suitable tree.

Sergeyenna and Hergiani are probably the most climbed routes on Chee Tor. They involve fine positions on perfect rock that demand a range of techniques. Hergiani, the right hand of the two, is perhaps the more strenuous of the routes and Sergeyenna the more perplexing, with some intimidating moves across the wall under the barrier of overhangs which guard the top of the crag. Despite its lower grade, Sergeyenna is the scene of many minor epics particularly for the second. The moves right require a positive approach and some good rope technique to prevent rope drag; lack of communication has ruined many a beautiful relationship.

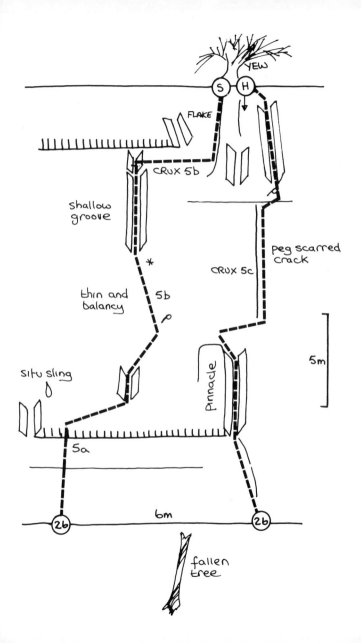

27: CHEE TOR GIRDLE (VS) 167m

Summary: A classic expedition in superb position, traversing the crag with increasing difficulty from right to left. The route follows the obvious break at two-thirds height. A good selection of long slings will be found useful for the numerous natural threads.

First Ascent: Chris Jackson and John Atkinson in 1964, just pipping Joe Brown et al. at the post.

Best Conditions: The break can weep after a wet spell but, being clear of the tree tops, the rock dries more rapidly than some of the ground-based routes. Late spring to early summer is probably the most reliable time. *See* Best Conditions for Route 20.

Approach: *See* introductory notes for Chee Tor. At the extreme right end of the crag is a small wall, cloaked on its right by vegetation. This is the first part of Chee Tor to be encountered when approaching from the upstream end; all routes described start left of this.

Starting Point: The girdle can be started at numerous points and indeed some parties choose to start further left as that end of the girdle contains the best climbing. However, traditionally, the route starts at the right end of the crag, at Doggone Groove, some 11m left of the small wall mentioned in the approach.

Descent: A mainly free abseil from a small tree below the break.

Chee Tor Girdle has become one of The Peak's classics, and it is not unusual to see two or three parties at work on a sunny afternoon. As with any girdle, it is important that climbers at each end of the rope are equally competent. This is especially important on Chee Tor, as a flying climber from the girdle could easily wipe out several parties on the routes underneath. Girdlers may find that they are required to share stances with climbers from the vertical routes below, most of which finish at the break.

The route grows progressively more exposed as one approaches the left end of the traverse, with the crux being just round a broad arête on the penultimate pitch. There are numerous natural threads along the break and the odd rusting peg, providing some excellent protection. The footholds are unfortunately becoming a little polished in places.

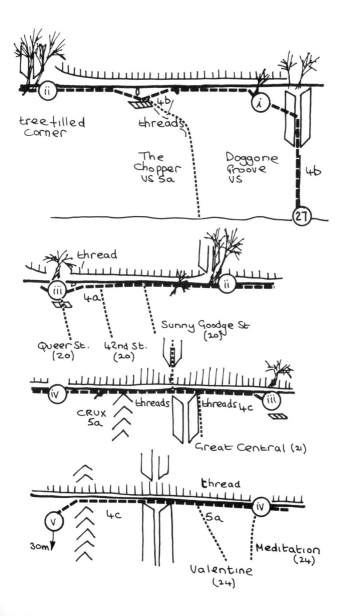

tree-filled corner

The Chopper VS 5a

Doggone Groove VS

4b

threads

27

thread

Queer St. (20)

42nd St. (20)

Sunny Goodge St (20)

4a

CRUX 5a

threads

threads 4c

Great Central (21)

thread

4c

5a

Meditation (24)

30m

Valentine (24)

Water-cum-Jolly Area

Water-cum-Jolly is the section of the Wye Valley which runs between Litton Mill and Cressbrook Mill. It is separated from the Chee Dale crags by the B6049 Tideswell to Buxton road and a short stretch of valley known as Miller's Dale. Miller's Dale contains a minor, surfaced road which runs alongside the river as far as the cottages at Litton Mill. Below here is Water-cum-Jolly and a concessionary footpath continues through the old mill buildings and along the riverside, past the crags, eventually regaining a road at Cressbrook Mill. The valley contains some difficult test-pieces and, in places, the rock is of uncertain quality but amongst these are several gems.

For all the routes described here, with the exception of Dragonflight on Rubicon Wall, the closest approach is from the Litton Mill end of the valley. The approach from Cressbrook Mill, though a little further, makes a very pleasant approach.

Approaches: For Litton Mill, take the small road which cuts acutely left from the B6049 in Miller's Dale at the foot of the hill from Tideswell. This is opposite a wooden 'cottage'. The road passes a pub, The Angler's Rest, then below the overhanging Raven Tor, with little of merit below E5, and eventually to the cottages at Litton Mill. **Do not park at the Mill.** Some 200m before the cottages, the valley widens at the foot of Tideswell Dale, where it is usually possible to park.

For Cressbrook Mill, follow a minor road from Litton Village (SK 165751) to Cressbrook, continue down the steep hill to where it is possible to park near the entrance to a builder's yard at the Mill.

For those without transport, the T208 bus from Sheffield to Hanley stops at The Angler's Rest in Miller's Dale and from Manchester the X67 Mansfield bus stops at Tideswell, from where a 2km walk down Tideswell Dale brings you out close to Litton Mill.

Accommodation: Camping – the valley is privately owned and camping is not allowed, the nearest campsite is at Blackwell (SK 123719).
Youth hostels – the youth hostel atop Raven Tor is ideally situated. Access to it is from the B6049 or from Miller's Dale.
Bivouacs – it is possible to bivouac in the caves at the foot of Raven Tor.
Hotels, b. & b. – these are numerous, and include The Monsal Head Hotel (SK 185715) and Upperdale Farm (SK 177722).

Services: Most things can be found in Tideswell. There is a phone box on the B6049 behind The Angler's Rest. A somewhat seasonal café can be found in Litton Mill, and Upperdale Farm in Monsal Dale (Below WCJ) also serves refreshments.

A Concise History: The first recorded ascent in Water-cum-Jolly was by Eric Byne and Clifford Moyer in 1933, and was aptly named The Gully, a rarely repeated route now reserved for the specialist. After that, the dale saw no recorded activity until the late 1950s when members of the Manchester Gritstone Club started their explorations. The main activists were Graham West, Barry Roberts, Jack Arrundale, B. Bamford and Malc Baxter and they were largely responsible for most of the routes which subsequently appeared in Graham West's *Limestone Guide* in 1961. During this period, most of the routes used considerable amounts of aid and few free climbs exceeded the VS category. This trend continued sporadically with mixed free and aid routes until the 1970s when the area started to receive attention from the new generation of free climbers. Ping, Ping Pong and Kunckle Knocker were free climbed by Keith Myhill in 1970 which was a notable breakthrough. However, it was not until 1975 when, amongst others, Tom Proctor, Geoff Birtles, Ernie Marshall and Al Evans arrived on the scene that things took off. The vicious cracks at the left end of Central Buttress were mainly climbed by this team but Proctor's greatest achievement here must be his ascent of Behemoth (E5 6b), the overhanging finger crack right of St Paul, and the hardest route on limestone in its day. During the summers of 1975 and 1976, Alan Sanderson and Mick Walsh developed many of the routes on Jackdaw Point, and Tom Proctor took the first free ascent of Fledgeling Flakes.

Since then, development has continued at a slow but steady pace. Many climbers have acquired a strong attachment to this beautiful spot over the years and left their calling cards; new routes have been excavated from amongst the ivy, loose blocks tumbled into the lake and aid points progressively eliminated from old routes. Jackson's discovery of Dragonflight focussed attention on the overhanging water-washed Rubicon Wall, now a popular area with 'the boys', which sports many modern tendon-snapping horrors, mostly E5 and above.

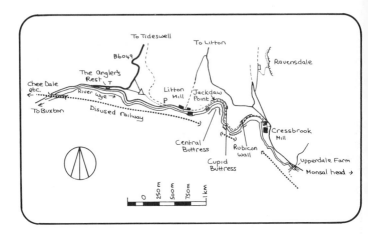

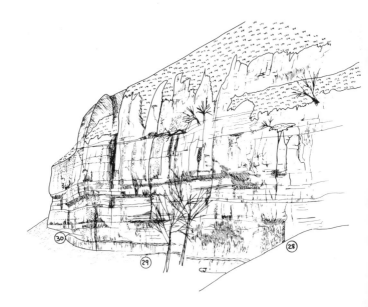

Bill Wintrip on Chee Tor Girdle, Chee Dale. (Photo: Chris Jackson.)

28: COLDITY CRACK & COLDITY GROOVE (E1, E2) 17m, 20m

Summary: Two pleasant climbs at the right-hand end of Central Buttress. The steep and shaky start of Coldity Groove adds more than a little spice to the route.

First Ascents: Coldity Crack – P. Bagnall and D. Murphy in 1964, as an aid route. The original start was freed by J. Campbell and C. Carey in 1976 to give the current line of Coldity Groove. The upper groove of Coldity Crack was added by Pete O'Donovan and Mark Stokes, also in 1976.

Best Conditions: Central Buttress faces north-west and gets afternoon sun only in the summer months. In winter the crag is hardly touched by the sun and can be a cold and draughty place. The crag does take some drainage from the extensive hillside above but is usually dry from May to September.

Approach: From Litton Mill, follow the concessionary footpath downstream to a small weir, level with the upstream end of Central Buttress. Wade the stream and ascend the slope to a small path along the foot of the crag. If the river is high, cross the footbridge above the mill and ascend the path to the disused railway line. Walk in the downstream direction to the closed-off tunnel, take the little path up the left side of the tunnel entrance, cross the fence and contour the hillside (carefully) until it is possible to scramble down to the riverside. Note, there is no right of way for this approach.

Starting Point: Coldity Crack – this is the square groove line high up at the right-hand end of the buttress where the ground rises. Start at a vague right-to-left slanting line leading to below the groove. Coldity Groove is the flared crack line to its left. Start below a shattered overhang 3m left of Coldity Crack.

Descent: Either by abseil from a suitable tree, or by wandering to the right for about 60m until it is possible to scramble down.

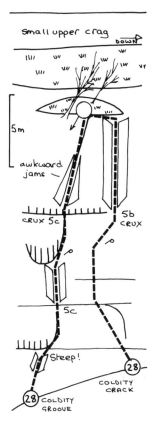

Small upper crag

DOWN

5m

awkward jams

CRUX 5c

5b CRUX

5c

Steep!

(28) COLDITY GROOVE

(28) COLDITY CRACK

29: KNUCKLE KNOCKER (E2) 39m

Summary: A thuggish start around a small overhang leads to enjoyable climbing up a steep groove.

First Ascent: Barry Roberts and Graham West in 1960, and graded VS exposed, A2. It is a classic from the pioneering days of limestone climbing. It was free climbed by Keith Myhill in the early 1970s.

Best Conditions: *See* Best Conditions for Route 28.

Approach: As for Route 28.

Starting Point: About half-way along the crag and above a narrow footledge is a long block roof at 5m. Start left of the thin crack which cuts the roof.

Descent: It is possible to abseil from one of the many trees but care should be taken not to dislodge rock onto parties below. It is better to follow the small path to the left to an easy descent beyond the buttress.

Crossing the roof at 5m is undoubtedly the crux of the route. There are good holds over the roof but it is not possible to spot them from below. The peg which shows just round the roof cons you into attempting a crossing here but the way on is a metre or so to the right. From large but flat holds, a good lock off is required to reach jugs and a possible belay ledge.

Most parties opt to run the climb out into one long pitch, which is safer but not essential. The groove of the second pitch looks comparatively easy but contains a couple of deceptively awkward moves past a ring peg of antique value only.

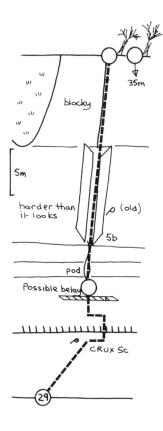

blocky

5m

harder than
it looks

(old)

5b

pod

Possible belay

CRUX 5c

35m

29

30: ST PAUL (E2) 36m

Summary: An excellent route giving some steep and sustained climbing in the first part of pitch 2. The crux moves can be well protected by wires.

First Ascent: D. Peck and Paul Nunn in June 1960, as an aid route, and graded S and A2. It was eventually freed by Andy Parkin and Pete O'Donovan in 1976.

Best Conditions: *See* Best Conditions for Route 28.

Approach: As for Route 28.

Starting Point: Towards the left end of the crag the path climbs a few metres to a low, shallow cave. St Paul starts a few metres right of this at a left-pointing flake line leading to ledges on the right.

Descent: Abseil from a suitable tree or climb the bank to a small path which can be followed left to an easy scramble descent.

This is the most popular route on the crag. The crux section starts with the second pitch; steep moves past an ancient peg lead to a good hold below the bulge and two more pegs. The crack above is well-worn for wires and some strenuous finger jamming brings a splendid jug to hand. Above, the going eases a little as things return to the vertical. The rickety chimney crack above should be treated with circumspection. Tree belays are set well back.

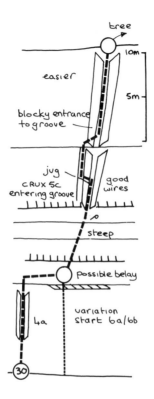

tree

10m

easier

5m

blocky entrance
to groove

jug

CRUX 5c
entering groove

good
wires

steep

possible belay

variation
start 6a/6b

4a

30

JACKDAW POINT

Jackdaw point lies opposite Central Buttress, on the true left bank of the River Wye, a few hundred metres downstream. In some respects it is the antithesis of Central Buttress for, where Central Buttress can be dark and austere, particularly in the winter, Jackdaw Point maintains a sunny aspect and is probably the most frequented piece of rock in Water-cum-Jolly.

ERITHACUS
ARMY DREAMERS

Mike Warwick on pitch 2 of Lyme Cryme (Route 40), High Tor, Matlock. (Photo: Chris Jackson.)

31: ERITHACUS & ARMY DREAMERS (E1, E2) 22m, 24m

Summary: Two enjoyable routes in delightful surroundings on the sunny side of the valley opposite Central Buttress. The start of Army Dreamers, though not technically difficult, is unprotected and requires a confident approach.

First Ascents: Erithacus – Alan Sanderson and Mick Walsh in 1977, with 1 point of aid, and freed later that year by J. Hesketh and D. Tait. Army Dreamers – Ron and Gill Fawcett in 1981.

Best Conditions: The routes dry quickly after rain, face south and receive much available sun. The crag, Jackdaw Point, is a pleasant venue even when other crags are damp and steeped in gloom.

Approach: From Litton Mill, walk downstream, past Central Buttress on the right and cross a small bridge over a tributary. Continue a few metres to a small track which leads steeply to the crag up the bank on the left.

Starting Point: Erithacus – below a set of thin cracks at the left end of the buttress. Army Dreamers – right of Erithacus and some 2m left of the lowest point of the buttress.

Descent: By abseil from the large tree at the top of the crag. Scramble descents are possible to the left (facing in) but are definitely not recommended.

The start of Erithacus is deceptively steep and it is not possible to attain a resting position until the ramp line is reached. Here, the character of the route changes and pleasant slabs lead to a good belay position. A few more strong pulls are required to gain the haven of the huge Ash tree. With careful rope work the two pitches can be led as one.

Army Dreamers takes a bold start to a peg above the thin horizontal break. Wire protection is then possible to where some steep moves on excellent holds land you on the ramp. Above, the start of the final wall, in contrast to the first section, is an awkward balance problem and is usually tackled from the right. With a little patience, wires can be arranged in the line of pockets on the traverse.

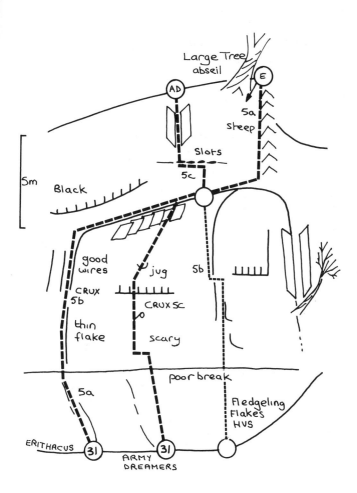

Large Tree
abseil

AD

E

5a
steep

Slots

5c

5m

Black

good
wires

jug

5b

CRUX
5b

CRUX 5c

thin
flake

scary

poor break

Fledgeling
Flakes
HVS

ERITHACUS

5a

31

31

ARMY
DREAMERS

32: PING & PING PONG (HVS, E1) 21m

Summary: Pleasant and well-protected crack climbs.

First Ascents: Ping – Graham West and Barry Roberts in 1959, reputedly using four pitons and no etriers. Ping Pong – graded HVS and climbed with 3 points of aid by unknown authors. Both were free climbed by Keith Myhill in 1970.

Best Conditions: The buttress takes little drainage, faces west and receives a fair amount of any available sunshine.

Approach: Cupid Buttress is on the left bank of the river, some 600m below Litton Mill. A track runs up into a well-worn scree gully, giving access to the right end of the buttress. Just downstream of the buttress is a pinnacle with a hole through it at half height.

Starting Points: The right end of the buttress is at a lower level to the rest. Ping starts at the left arête of this lower section. Ping Pong starts out of the small tree right of Ping and below the obvious thin flake crack.

Descent: Traverse right into the easy gully.

Two sustained and interesting routes. Protection is particularly good on Ping and although runners are a little spaced on Ping Pong they arrive when most needed – on the steep upper section.

PING ㉜   PING PONG ㉜

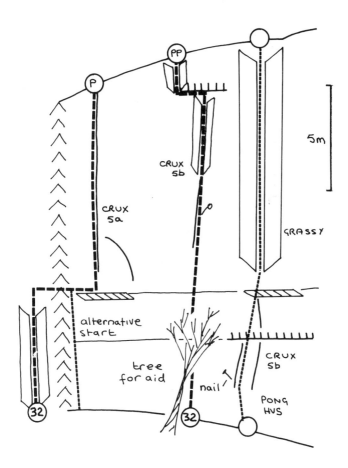

PP

P

CRUX
5a

CRUX
5b

5m

GRASSY

alternative
start

tree
for aid

nail

CRUX
5b

PONG
HVS

32

32

33: DRAGONFLIGHT (E3) 20m

Summary: An intimidating but delightful little route on immaculate rock. It is now becoming polished.

First Ascent: Chris Jackson, Rod Haslam and Dave Sant in 1976. It was originally graded HVS for which the author has since received considerable flak.

Best Conditions: The route faces south but the upper crack can remain wet for some time after a damp spell due to drainage from the jungle.

Approach: Rubicon Wall is usually approached from the lower, Cress-brook Mill end of the valley. From the road, walk through the builder's yard and through a gate to the lake. The long wall above the lakeside path is Rubicon Wall, which contains many hard modern problems that are popular with 'the boys'. From Litton Mill take a pleasant 1.5km stroll downstream.

Starting Point: Towards the left end of the buttress below a flake curving to the right.

Descent: Walk back through the jungle to a small track which is followed left to a steep descent.

The first problem is to obtain a standing position on the thin ledge at about 4m, which is more difficult than the audience on the path would have you believe. The ledge also takes the protection for the next trying little move. Faith and friction allow better holds to come to hand just as the climber-to-runner distance equals runner to path. A good ledge permits some composure to be regained before the final short sharp (but better-protected) crack.

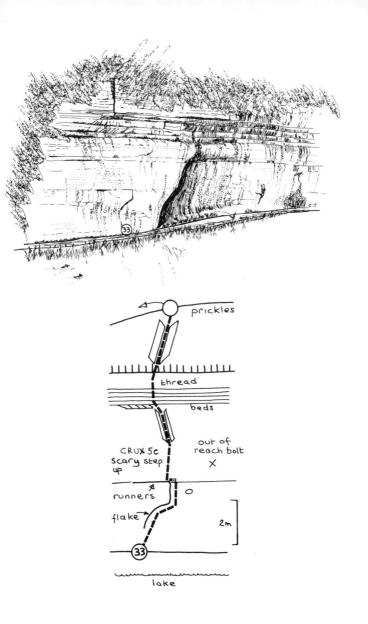

prickles

thread

beds

CRUX 5c
scary step
up

out of
reach bolt
X

runners

flake

O

2m

33

lake

Matlock Area

The Matlock area crags lie in the south-east corner of The Peak District, between Matlock in the north and Cromford village in the south, along the banks of the River Derwent. The crags are of a high-quality pocketed limestone, generally steep but often with surprisingly good holds. Four crags are covered in this guide: Pic Tor is the smallest but contains many well protected but fingery climbs; High Tor, possibly The Peak's premier crag, holds many difficult and classic climbs in superb position; Wildcat Crags and Willersley Castle Rocks are slightly less demanding but very worth while. Pic Tor and Willersley Castle Rocks face north while High Tor and Wildcat Crags face west.

Matlock and Matlock Bath are busy holiday towns and have, among other things, a cable-car, show caves, amusement parks and arcades, souvenir shops, chippies, lots of motor cyclists and even more people. However, the crags are not quite as crowded as the towns and they contain a high population of superb climbs.

Approaches: Matlock lies on the A6 trunk road and is easily reached by bus from Derby, Chesterfield, Bakewell and Buxton. Matlock and Matlock Bath also have railway stations. A more detailed approach description for each crag is given in the appropriate section.

Accommodation: Camping – at sites about 2.5km north-east of Matlock off the A623, and south, close to the A6 at SK 330550.
Youth hostels – in Matlock, up the steep hill from the roundabout.
Hotels, b. & b. – numerous hotels and pubs offer accommodation in the area.
Bivouacs – dotted along the river bank between Matlock and Matlock Bath are a number of park shelters which might be used in an emergency. The practice would undoubtedly be frowned upon by the local authorities. High Tor has a ledge system some 20m up, below the overhangs of Castellan, which would afford some shelter to the aspiring Alpinist. Take care, there has been a death from rolling out of bed here. At Willersley Castle Rocks, the overhang below Great Corner would provide some shelter.

Services: Matlock and Matlock Bath have most things. There is a mountain rescue post at Matlock.

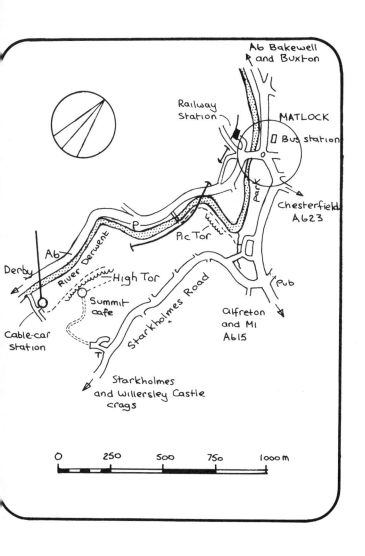

PIC TOR

Pic Tor is a fingery little crag of excellent pocketed limestone. Prior to
1980, Pic Tor contained only a few nondescript aid routes but it was
rediscovered by Gary Gibson and friends who were responsible for most
of the subsequent routes. The crag faces north at a bend in the river at
the downstream end of Hall Leys Park in Matlock. It is sheltered, close to
a park footpath, one minute from your car (if you can get a place to park)
and has been described as an outdoor gymnasium. There is also a sandy
beach by the river if you get bored of cranking up on *les monodoigt*.
Protection is generally good, mainly smaller wires plus small slings for
natural threads – some of which may be found *in situ*. Regard these with
suspicion; sadly some of the threads have been vandalized.

Approaches: From the roundabout in Matlock, take the A615 along by
the park for some 500m. Parking is allowed here and there, and also on
the right at the end of the park. Cross the bridge and walk along the
footpath past two scruffy-looking crags on the left, to Pic Tor. For those
prepared to pay for parking, take the A6 south, under the railway bridge
to a car-park on the left. Cross the footbridge and walk upstream. The
crag is on the right.

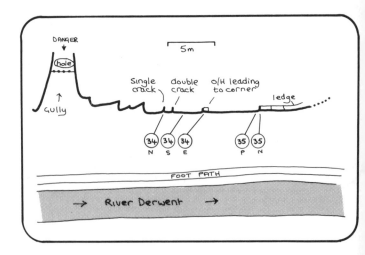

Mike Browell on Robert Brown (Route 39), High Tor, Matlock.
(Photo: Chris Jackson.)

34: NOSFERATU, SILENUS & ERASMUS (E2, E2, E2) 23m

Summary: Three routes which give a good introduction to the style of climbing on Pic Tor and, to some extent, High Tor as well. None of the routes are high in their grade, the rock is generally sound and good protection can be arranged. The upper crack of Nosferatu provides the most difficult problem of the three routes. The less bold may find themselves clutching a runner.

First Ascents: Nosferatu – Gary Gibson, Derek Beetlestone and Alison Hargreaves in May 1980. Silenus – Gary Gibson in November 1983, unseconded. Erasmus – Gary Gibson and Phil Gibson in June 1980.

Best Conditions: The crag dries quite rapidly given half a chance.

However, it is worth bearing in mind that the climbs face north and the pockets can retain moisture even when the crag appears to be dry.

Approach: *See* Approaches under Pic Tor.

Starting Point: Nosferatu – at a prominent flake crack just right of an arête in the central section of the crag. Silenus – below the centre of the wall about 2m further right, and right again. Erasmus – below a shallow groove leading to an overhang.

Descent: Abseil from one of the many trees.

These routes form an interesting trilogy, each containing different aspects of the same game. Nosferatu lures you into thinking that the route is going to be a walk over, then traps you on the upper wall. Runner placements are plentiful but holds are not, and staying in position while you sort out the appropriate wire for that perfect crack in front of your nose, can be difficult. Silenus has a far more civilized character, involving elegant moves between pockets, stepping into unlikely-looking territory only to find a perfect little incut, and *in situ* threads to keep you comfortable. The crux is probably on the upper wall but this does not last long; the E1 that thinks it is an E2. Erasmus is perhaps the boldest of the three and the shallow groove is deceptively awkward, but not as awkward as the moves left to join Silenus. However, good protection can be arranged up on the right to protect the moves and, once launched across the wall, good holds soon come within reach.

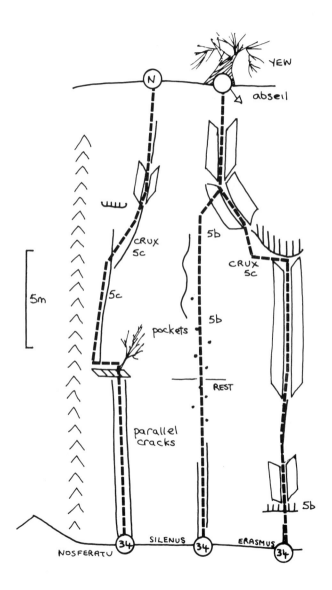

N

YEW

abseil

5m

CRUX
5c

5c

5b

pockets

5b

CRUX
5c

REST

parallel
cracks

5b

NOSFERATU   SILENUS   ERASMUS

34   34   34

35: NEUROSIS & PROGNOSIS (E3, E3) 20m

Summary: Fine, steep climbing up the pocketed wall at the right end of the crag. Although neither route is high in its grade, Neurosis may be found more difficult for climbers of short stature. Both routes are fairly well protected but beware of wires behind expandable (expendable!) flakes. Small wires will generally be found useful along with a few clippers.

First Ascents: Prognosis – Gary Gibson and A. Hudson in November 1983. Neurosis – Gary Gibson in November 1983, unseconded.

Best Conditions: *See* Best Conditions for Route 34.

Approach: *See* Approaches under Pic Tor.

Starting Point: Both routes start from a ledge at 2.5m, near the right end of the crag.

Descent: It is strongly recommended that you abseil.

Starting with the easier of the two, Prognosis is probably the best route on the crag and covers some unlikely-looking territory. It weaves its way right and then left from crack to flake and back again, with adequate though not excessive protection. Some care is required to ensure that rope drag does not pull the runners out. It is just possible to get a one-hand off rest towards the top where the route moves left. The route finishes at a bunch of slings and bolts where you can take a hanging belay or lower to the ground, taking care not to damage the belay sling. Neurosis is a tough little cookie, requiring some determined fingers and neat footwork. It is also easy to make a wrong move, whence failure will almost certainly ensue. After the initial steep wall, the route trends left towards an inviting gangway and, although it is possible to reach this from below, it is classed as cheating as it avoids the crux of the route. Summons all and, from good holds below the ramp, aim for the sky and for jugs which lead to the bolt belays.

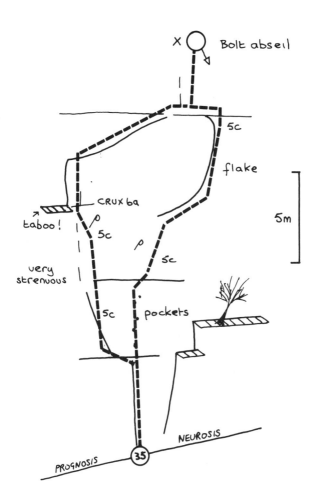

X ○ Bolt abseil

5c

flake

5m

CRUX 6a

taboo!

ρ

5c

ρ

very
strenuous

5c

5c

pockets

NEUROSIS

PROGNOSIS

35

HIGH TOR

High Tor is probably The Peak's premier crag, its gleaming white walls hang above the River Derwent and dominate the A6 between the 'Matlocks'. Here the climber will find some of the best climbs on Peak limestone. Although little more than 50m at its highest, High Tor has the feel of a big cliff and it is easy to become intimidated by it, particularly on a first visit. The crag is quick drying and starts to catch any available sun at around midday and can in fact become uncomfortably hot on still summer days. Its elevated position also means that it can be exposed to the wind.

Approaches: High Tor lies on private land and can be approached from above or below. The normal approach is from below and the start is marked by the cable-car station which has to be passed to gain access to the grounds. Free parking is possible in the lay-bys close to the iron footbridge, and there is a Pay and Display car-park in Matlock Bath railway station. Once in the grounds, follow rough tracks up the hillside to a well-used track, contouring the hillside to the left.

An alternative for the decadently mobile is to follow the A615 Alfreton road from the roundabout in Matlock for about 1km, then turn right up a long hill, signposted Starkholmes. At the crest of the hill, by a phone box, turn right along a track which eventually brings you out by the summit café, where there is a fee for parking. It is then possible to make an exposed abseil from the tree at the top of Darius (50m) to the foot of the crag or follow a footpath cut into the rock on the left side of the crag (facing out), then scramble down through the trees.

Bob Conway on Sundance Wall (Route 84), The Terrace, Malham Cove. (Photo: Chris Jackson.)

36: ORIGINAL ROUTE (HVS) 39m

Summary: Superb climbing up the thin groove on the right of the main face. Steep and fingery, never easy but protectable and in tremendous position. Despite its uninspiring name, Original Route is one of the great classics of High Tor, and is now becoming rather polished. A few extra clippers may be found useful for the odd peg runner.

First Ascent: Possibly climbed free by Steve Read and Steve Hirst in 1958, but probably with some aid (details are a little confused). It was definitely climbed free by 1961.

Best Conditions: High Tor takes little drainage and dries rapidly. However, the exposed setting of the crag can make it a cold and draughty venue during the winter months.

Approach: *See* Approaches under High Tor.

Starting Point: Original Route is the groove formed between the slabby main face of High Tor and the much steeper right-hand side. Start some 10m up at a small tree below the groove.

Descent: From the top of the route, facing inland, turn right and follow the tourist path cut into the cliff until it is possible to scramble easily down through the trees to the footpath that runs below the face.

A tremendous climb and a 'must' for any visiting party. Original Route is steep and somewhat fingery and, despite being a groove line, much of the route is face climbing. It is possible to start directly behind the tree at a steep little crack, which is part of Flakey Wall (E4), but it is easier to move 3m to the left and take a rising traverse rightwards into the groove. Good footwork will pay dividends, and in places it is possible to bridge out onto the right wall of the groove to take the weight off your arms. There are numerous placements for medium-to-large wires and several peg runners.

   The belay is on a fine long ledge, where two finishes are possible; either direct (which is hard) or traverse right for 4m and climb up through the bulges to the top.

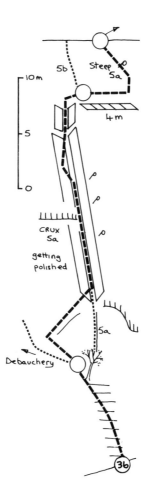

37: DEBAUCHERY (E1) 45m

Summary: Probably the most popular climb on High Tor. The route takes a rising traverse crossing the main face from right to left and covers some fascinating territory. Holds are often surprisingly good but a certain expertise in rope work and route-finding can be an advantage.

First Ascent: Chris Jackson and John Atkinson in 1965. This was the first essentially free climb across the main face of High Tor. The original line differs slightly from that now taken, a pendule was used to cross the first section into Darius, requiring some alarming rope work and the necessity to climb part of Darius without close runners. Pete Livesey and John Sheard probably climbed the current connection in 1967.

Best Conditions: As for Route 36.

Approach: *See* Approaches under High Tor.

Starting Point: As for Route 36.

Descent: Either make a 50m abseil from the tree overhanging the summit of High Tor, having consideration for climbers below or, facing inland, walk right and follow the tourist path until it is possible to scramble easily down through the trees to the path along the bottom of the face.

A splendid trip, crossing some unlikely-looking territory at a reasonable standard. The start is steep but remarkable holds repeatedly materialize, which soon lead to the rickety pillar and the stance. This is a popular venue and a common crossing point for many routes, and it is not unusual to be sharing with other parties at this point. From here the route becomes complex and the degree of difficulty involved in crossing a small groove below some holes very much depends upon how it is tackled: too high or too low and you are in 5c territory but, if you get it just right, a brilliant little jug comes straight to hand. The route continues steeply left around a nose above the huge overhangs of Castellan, although fortunately you can not see them. Eventually it is possible to climb straight up and, if you are lucky, there will be time for a cup of tea at the summit café and round again.

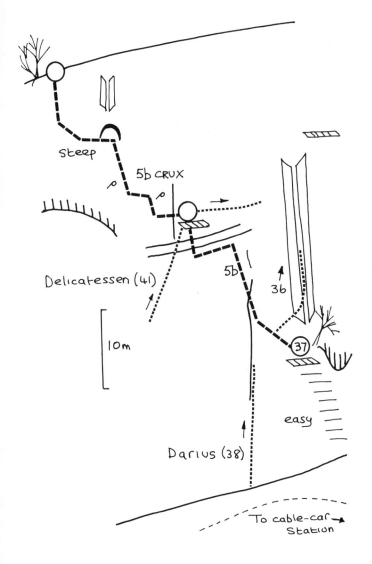

steep

5b CRUX

Delicatessen (41)

10m

5b

3b

37

easy

Darius (38)

To cable-car
Station

38: DARIUS (E2) 51m

Summary: A sustained and technical route giving absorbing climbing in superb situations with good protection. Pitch 2 can be taken as one run out, in which case extra wires in the middle sizes and a few extra slings may be found useful.

First Ascent: Oliver Woolcock, Clive Rowland and Paul Nunn in 1963 as an aid route, and first climbed free in 1967 by Pete Livesey.

Best Conditions: As for Route 36.

Approach: *See* Approaches under High Tor.

Starting Point: Start at a prominent groove 5m right of a large tree at the base of the cliff.

Descent: As for Route 37.

Fifty-metre ropes will be found useful on the second pitch, although it is possible to take a hanging belay where Delicatessen (41) traverses towards Original Route (36). It is far better as one fabulous pitch, following first thin flakes and then a groove to a tiny ledge below the final, apparently blank section, with the top tantalizingly close. For many years a bolt was used as aid at this point but eventually a climber fell off and took the bolt with him. It was subsequently replaced but by then the moves had become established as free. The easiest finish, but probably still the technical crux of the route, is to climb up and then left into a hanging corner. It is also possible to make a harder finish by climbing direct or to the right. Belay on the tree on the edge of the crag.

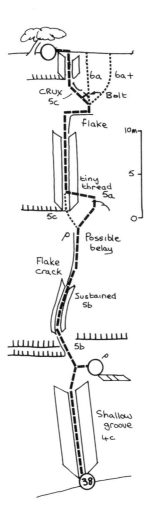

6a 6a+

CRUX
5c

Bolt

flake

10m

tiny
thread
5a

5

5c

0

P   Possible
     belay

Flake
crack

Sustained
5b

5b

P

Shallow
groove
4c

38

39: ROBERT BROWN (E3) 52m

Summary: Intimidating climbing up the face to the left of Darius. It does not have a high technical grade, but the traverse above the bulge on pitch 1 requires a certain amount of commitment and the ability to climb well above your runners.

First Ascent: Arnis Strapcans and Jerry Frost in November 1974. This was originally an aid route called Bastion Wall, climbed by Peter Biven and Trevor Peck, and was renamed in memory of Arnis's climbing partner who was killed in a climbing accident on Gogarth, Anglesey. Arnis tragically disappeared while soloing the Brenva Face of Mont Blanc.

Best Conditions: As for Route 36.

Approach: *See* Approaches under High Tor.

Starting Point: At a prominent groove behind the tree at the foot of the crag, left of Darius.

Descent: As for Route 37.

Although given a higher adjectival grade than Darius, the route is technically easier, but it does require a somewhat bolder approach. Above the peg, a bulge is climbed and some committing and unprotected moves right are required to reach the haven of a good flake. You are only 3 or 4m above good protection but it can feel like a lot more if confidence or strength start to fade. Beyond this the route is pure enjoyment, with alternative finishes, both at 5b.

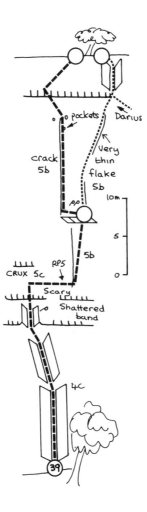

Darius

pockets

crack
5b

Very
thin
flake
5b

RP5

CRUX 5c

Scary

Shattered
band

4c

39

10m

5

0

40: LYME CRYME (E3) 46m

Summary: A difficult and splendid route climbing the face right of the caves of Castellan. The first pitch is deceptively steep with a serious air about it. Above this, wonderful climbing up the steep, cracked face leads to the top. A standard rack, plus extra clippers for the pegs and a few slings, may be found useful.

First Ascent: Steve Bancroft and Adey Hubbard in October 1975. The route boasts the first free climbing bolt in The Peak. Always a dubious fixture, it eventually fell out, probably under the effects of gravity, to be replaced by one only marginally better.

Best Conditions: As for Route 36.

Approach: *See* Approaches under High Tor.

Starting Point: Left of the tree at the foot of the crag, at a black, scarred groove leading to bulges.

Descent: Walk right to the summit of the crag and the abseil tree or continue right and descend via the tourist path, as for Route 37.

A fine test-piece fitting into the middle of its grade. The hardest moves are in the initial groove and are well protected but the crux is probably overcoming fear above the disgusting-looking bolt below the bulge on pitch 1. However, the moves above the bolt are easier than they look and there is usually an *in situ* sling from an old ice peg which is within reach from good holds. Above the bulge, the crag tilts back to the right side of vertical and the second pitch follows cracks and flakes to give some well-protected and very enjoyable climbing, crossing Debauchery at the holes into an airy finishing groove.

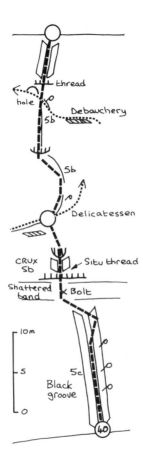

41: DELICATESSEN (E2) 60m

Summary: A counter diagonal to Debauchery, with an intimidating start out of the caves of Castellan and a technical finish into the top of Original Route. Slightly harder than its counter route, it is nevertheless very worth while as it covers some impressive territory.

First Ascent: Pitches 1 and 2 – Chris Jackson and John Atkinson in October 1965. Pitch 3 – Jack Street and Ed Ward-Drummond in October 1968. The lapse between the ascents of these two parts of the route aptly demonstrates the changes in attitudes and pressures for new routes over the last twenty years.

Best Conditions: As for Route 36.

Approach: *See* Approaches under High Tor.

Starting Point: Climb the first pitch of Skylight (42) and then traverse right along ledges beneath the overhangs to peg and nut belays in the caves of Castellan.

Descent: The route finishes at the last pitch of Route 36. Therefore descend in the same way as for this.

The start takes the lower break out of the right-hand end of the caves. It can be quite scary, with some long strides, which are fairly well protected but remember your second, as there are some awkward moves. It is difficult to communicate across this pitch and some sort of pre-arranged signal for 'taking in' may be useful. Once round the corner, the oppressive overhangs are left behind and it is possible to take a belay as for Lyme Cryme. Some parties choose to press on to the ledge on Debauchery but this makes communications impossible and rope drag is almost inevitable. The traverse right from the Debauchery ledge is in complete contrast with the first part of the route, being delicate and requiring some technical footwork to gain the top of Original Route, the finish for the two routes being in the same place.

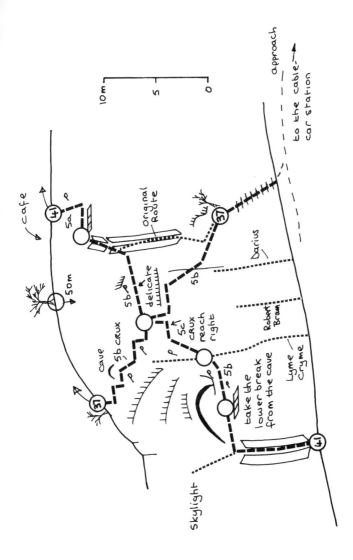

42: SKYLIGHT (VS) 42m

Summary: A traditional climb with a finish in fine position, now becoming very polished. The route takes the prominent right-facing crack and corner at the left end of the ledges leading to the caves of Castellan.

First Ascent: Steeped in tradition, a Joe Brown classic from one of his rare visits to limestone, in 1957.

Best Conditions: A little dampness may persist below the final chimney.

Approach: *See* Approaches under High Tor.

Starting Point: At the corner system, directly below the prominent chimney and left of the huge caves.

Descent: Scramble up to the top of the cliff and follow this, bearing right, to descend by the tourist path cut into the cliff, until it is possible to scramble down through the trees to the footpath that runs below the face.

Pleasant climbing up the corner leads to the left end of the prominent ledge system which leads to the caves of Castellan, and gives good views of this impressive section of cliff. Pitch 2 starts with a well-polished jamming crack but real holds soon come within reach.

Gaining the chimney crack probably constitutes the crux but good protection can usually be arranged before launching out.

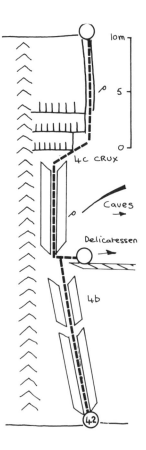

43: HIGHLIGHT (HVS) 45m

Summary: The route takes the prominent groove leading to an obvious roof which is tackled by traversing left and making some sensational moves into the easier finishing groove. Care should be taken with rope management and long extenders may be required for the runners under the roof to avoid desperate rope drag.

First Ascent: Doug Scott and Steve Read in 1964, with 3 points of aid. The first free ascent is unknown.

Best Conditions: Dries fairly quickly.

Approach: *See* Approaches under High Tor.

Starting Point: Below the groove, capped by an overhang, left of the chimney of Skylight (42).

Descent: As for Route 42.

Old pegs around the overlap in the groove betray the site of at least one of the old aid sections. The groove finishes at the roof where it is possible to take a secure hanging belay, if you like that kind of thing. The next few moves can be intimidating but are technically reasonable; the roof blocks the view above and the wall below cuts away out of sight leaving you with a wonderful sense of isolation. The only reasonable option is to edge out left, across the wall to the hanging arête in an exhilarating position and into the easier finishing groove.

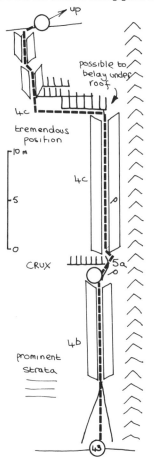

44: M1 (E2) 35m

Summary: A tremendous line and a justifiably popular route, covering some steep and impressive terrain on the left wing of High Tor. A few extra long slings or tapes may be found useful.

First Ascent: Doug Scott and C. Davies in 1961, graded HVS and A1. Aid was reduced to 1 point at the end of the traverse by Tom Proctor and Keith Myhill in 1968 and it was completely free climbed by Ed Ward-Drummond in 1969.

Best Conditions: The cracks below the roof sometimes weep after prolonged rain.

Approach: *See* Approaches under High Tor. Follow the path below the crags past the High Tor Gully.

Starting Point: M1 is on the left wing of High Tor, which is to the left of High Tor Gully. From High Tor Gully, follow the path below the crag, bearing left, until you are below an overhanging, stratified wall, topped by a left-facing corner leading to a large roof system (*see* diagram). Scramble up to belays below the corner.

Descent: It is possible to abseil from any of several small trees along the top of the crag but it is far better to walk up to the café for a pot of tea and then descend from the summit of the crag by the tourist path, as for Original Route (36).

For many years, M1 was graded HVS and was famous for its leader falls. Now that the grade has been rationalized, it sits comfortably within its grade but has given many a HVS leader a very bad time. It is an atmospheric route in superb position. The initial corner is steeper than it appears, and the juggy start soon changes to smaller holds requiring a determined and calculated approach. There is a peg out on the left, half way up the corner, which is easily missed and usually very welcome. From the sloping belay ledge in the corner, the route traverses left with increasing difficulty and in intimidating position, the objective being to gain the hidden groove at the end of the overhangs. The crux is a steep and committing move into the hidden groove. Good protection can be arranged but the position is tiring and a slip could leave you with good views of Ron Fawcett's Roadrunner (E6). Above, it is plain sailing but watch out for rope drag round the overhang.

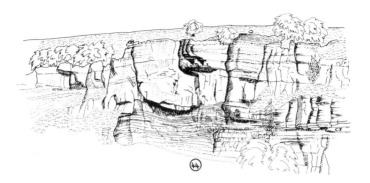

(44)

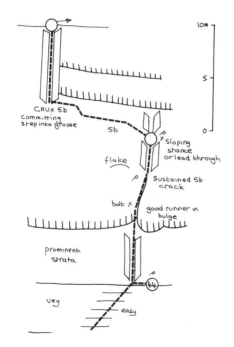

10m

5

0

CRUX 5b
committing
step into groove

5b

flake

Sustained 5b
crack

Sloping
stance
or lead through

good runner in
bulge

bolt x

prominent
strata

(44)

veg

easy

WILDCAT CRAGS

The Crags form a line of wooded buttresses facing across the River Derwent to Matlock Bath and the A6. The routes tend to be shorter and less demanding than those on the neighbouring High Tor and are a popular venue for climbers active at intermediate grades. The rock is generally good and the crag faces west, getting all the available afternoon sun where the buttresses rise above the tree level.

Approaches: Please read this section. The buttresses covered in this guide lie in the private grounds of Willersley Castle, owned by Wesley Methodist Guild Holidays. Access has been problematical in the past and approaches to the crags have been negotiated with the landowners who are uneasy about climbers.

Motorists going to Main Crag or High Crag are advised to use one of the Pay and Display car-parks as police and traffic wardens are vigilant in Matlock Bath. The easiest approach is from the pavilion, a fancy-looking building next to the fishpond and overlooking the pleasure gardens. Walk down through the gardens, cross the new bridge, turn right along the river bank and take a zigzag path which leads up the hillside, just short of a wall. Beyond the wall is private land. **Do not use the riverside path.** The first routes described here are on The Main Crag which starts beyond (downstream of) the wall. Ascend the hillside to the foot of the crag and use only the upper path for access to the routes. Climbers are also asked to keep Anglo-Saxon expletives to a minimum. Remember that the land is owned by a religious establishment and they are uneasy about climbers having access to the castle grounds. Take care, offence could lose us access to the crags.

Approach to Upper Tor: Climbers are asked to call at Willersley Castle to seek permission. To find this, continue through Matlock Bath, pass a right turn to Cromford and turn left down Station Road. There is parking on the right by the Cromford Canal. Walk in the same direction, cross the river and follow the drive to the castle on the left. Once permission has been granted, walk past the castle and follow a small overgrown drive up and right to the crag which is well screened by trees.

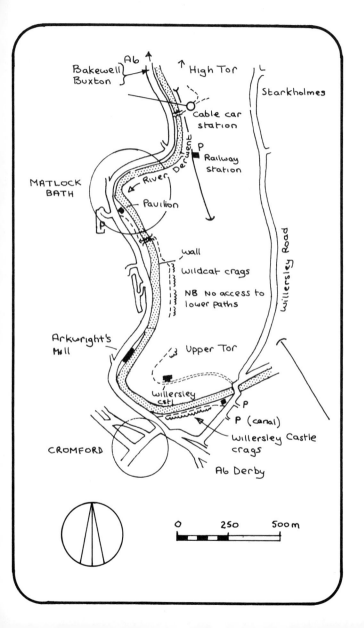

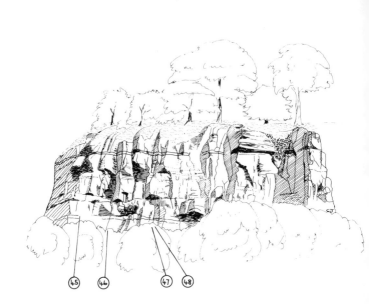

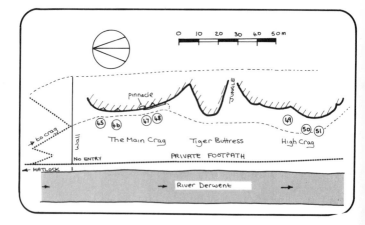

45: CATASTROPHE GROOVES (HVS) 38m

Summary: An excellent route giving a fine introduction to climbing on Wildcat Crags.

First Ascent: Doug Scott and Steve Read, possibly in the early 1960s, using 3 points of aid.

Best Conditions: During periods of unsettled weather, the bottom 3–6m of Wildcat Crags can be disturbingly slimy.

Approach: *See* Approaches under Wildcat Crags.

Starting Point: At a well-worn patch below a clean-cut groove, towards the left end of The Main Crag.

Descent: If you are using double ropes, descent can be accomplished by abseil, but it is easier to walk back and left (facing in) to a descent path.

The crux of the route is usually found to be at the steep section between the two grooves on pitch 2. There is a peg off to the right at this point which can be clipped if one of the ropes is left unclipped in the groove below. Belay on the tree hanging over the edge.

46: LYON ROUTE (E1) 40m

Summary: A popular route with an exciting second pitch. Protection is a little spaced in the upper reaches and a certain determination is required for a couple of moves.

First Ascent: Steve Read and W. McLoughlin in June 1963.

Best Conditions: As for Route 45.

Approach: *See* Approaches under Wildcat Crags.

Starting Point: Below shallow grooves and cracks in a grey wall, leading to an obvious stance in a large left-facing corner.

Descent: By abseil or walk back and left (facing in) to a descent path.

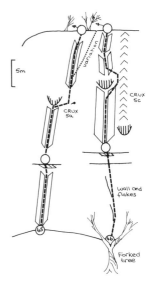

The apparently easy-looking corner on pitch 2 is harder than it looks. There is a good placement for a camming device in a pocket below the crux and those with a long reach may fix something above. A few non-stop moves are required to overcome the bulge which seems to be developing something of a polish.

47: BROKEN TOE GROOVE (VS) 40m

Summary: Fine climbing, particularly in the upper sections. Protection can be a little spaced in the starting crack unless you happen to own a very large camming device.

First Ascent: The current line is a combination of two older routes. Pitch 1 – Doug Scott and I. Thorby in 1963. Pitch 2 – Des Hadlum and Dennis Gray in 1960.

Best Conditions: The upper reaches dry fairly quickly but the starting crack can hold some dampness.

Approach: *See* Approaches under Wildcat Crags.

Starting Point: Right of the black corner of Lyon Route (46) is a small pinnacle with a narrow ledge on its right and a wide crack above it. Start at the crack.

Descent: Either abseil or a better idea is to walk back to the path and follow this, bearing left, to the foot of the crag.

Pitch 1 usually requires an ungainly thrutch to pass the small roof. Experts in the art of Yosemite off-widths will have no problem here, although most parties resort to a knee jam and holds deep-hidden within the crack. The pleasant upper pitch is in splendid position which makes the route well worth climbing. The protection situation rapidly improves once the crux is passed.

48: JACKDAW GROOVES (VS) 40m

Summary: An excellent route with some fine situations, giving a good introduction to limestone climbing.

First Ascent: Pitch 1 – D. Meadows and T. Watts. Pitch 2 – Doug Scott and R. Gillies in 1963.

Best Conditions: The upper reaches dry fairly quickly but the starting crack can hold some dampness.

Approach: *See* Approaches under Wildcat Crags.

Starting Point: A few metres right of the small pinnacle at a well-cracked groove.

Descent: Either abseil or walk back to the path which runs along the top. Follow this left and down to the foot of the crag.

A popular outing and rightly so. Good protection can be arranged for most of the route and the upper crack gives some fine exposed situations despite its modest grade. An ability to hand and finger jam might prove advantageous.

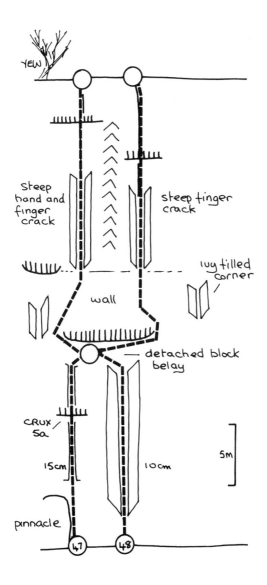

YEW

steep hand and finger crack

steep finger crack

ivy filled corner

wall

detached block belay

CRUX 5a

15cm

10cm

5m

pinnacle

47 48

49: GOLDEN YARDSTICK (VS) 44m

Summary: Worth climbing if only for its superb and unlikely-looking upper pitch.

First Ascent: Tom Proctor, Al Evans and Keith Myhill in 1975.

Best Conditions: During periods of unsettled weather, the bottom 3–10m of the route can be disturbingly slimy.

Approach: *See* Approaches under Wildcat Crags.

Starting Point: At the left-hand side of High Crag (*see* Map) is a pinnacle. Start to the right of this, below and to the right of a cave topped by a hanging rib.

Descent: Either abseil or a better idea is to walk back to the path and follow this, bearing left, to the foot of the crag.

Usually climbed for its fine second pitch. The unlikely-looking rib above the cave contains some amazing holds which give exhilarating climbing where climbing looks impossible.

50: GREAT CLEFT & TUT'S ANOMALOUS (E1, E1) 40m

Summary: Two steep upper pitches on excellent holds. Some larger nuts or camming devices may be found useful on pitch 2 of Tut's and a degree of tenacity for the classic thrutch, Great Cleft. Essential Wildcat for any competent visiting party.

First Ascents: Tut's Anomalous – originally climbed with 2 aid points but the authors and date are unknown. It was free climbed in 1977. Great Cleft – Doug Scott and Steve Read in 1963 using 3 points of aid, and freed by parties unknown before 1981.

Best conditions: The cracks on pitch 2 of Tut's can weep after a prolonged wet spell. Great Cleft is also prone to seepage.

Approach: *See* Approaches under Wildcat Crags.

Starting Point: High Crag is characterized by the prominent crack of Great Cleft in the upper reaches of the crag. For Tut's Anomalous, start at a shallow groove 3m right of a pedestal with a tree growing out of it, which leads to a rising, leftwards traverse line. Great Cleft starts 3m to the right again, at a thin crack below a shallow groove.

Descent: By abseil from the large tree, or walk back and left to the descent gully.

Two steep routes giving some exhilarating climbing. With Tut's, the grade of the climb is directly proportional to the number of runners you need to fix in the upper cracks of pitch 2, which can on occasions also be the source of a small spring. Great Cleft is a classic struggle with some awkward and overhanging jamming moves, though the pitch can be well protected by wires and camming devices, if you can hang on to place them.

51: LYNX & SPHYNX (HS, VS)
46m, 40m

Summary: Two pleasant routes in good position weaving their way up the buttress at a reasonable standard.

First Ascent: Lynx – Steve Read and S. Hunt in 1958. Sphynx – Steve Read and W. McLaughlin in 1963.

Best Conditions: The start for these two routes, common to both, is slabby and can retain some dampness.

Approach: *See* Approaches under Wildcat Crags.

Starting Point: Just to the right of a pedestal with a fallen tree, and below the black bulges right of Great Cleft.

Descent: Either find a suitable tree for abseil or a better idea is to follow the summit path, bearing left, down to the foot of the crag.

Two enjoyable routes of quite different character. Lynx follows a series of ledges interspaced with awkward problems, with good views of the harder routes around. Sphynx sneaks off to the right and finds some exposed rock on the back of the rib which forms the right half of Great Cleft.

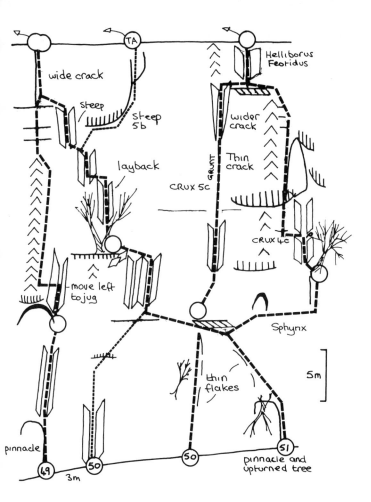

wide crack

steep

Steep
5b

layback

move left
to jug

pinnacle

TA

Helliborus
Feotidus

wider
crack

Thin
crack

GRUNT

CRUX 5c

CRUX 4c

Sphynx

5m

thin
flakes

pinnacle and
upturned tree

49   50   50   51

3m

52: LIBERTY CAP & GREAT CRACK (E2, E2) 18m

Summary: Two high-quality exercises in steep crack climbing on Upper Tor. The rock is excellent and the routes highly protectable and situated in pleasant surroundings. The crag catches the afternoon sun, and the flat top makes a pleasant little picnic spot.

First Ascents: Great Crack – Doug Scott and Steve Read in July 1963 using 3 points of aid. Liberty Cap – Ted Wells in the late 1970s.

Best Conditions: Both routes dry fairly rapidly, although in summer the trees tend to shade the lower part of the crag.

Approach: Important. Approach via Willersley Castle. *See* Approaches for Upper Tor under Wildcat Crags.

Starting Points: Liberty Cap – below a small roof at the left end of the front face. Great Crack – below the obvious central crack.

Descent: Walk back through the jungle and down to the right.

Two short but memorable climbs well deserving their classic status despite the lack of stature. Liberty Cap comes out fighting immediately you leave the ground. It is tiring to fix the runners round the roof and often climbers are lowered ignominiously to the ground on their first attempt. Deceptively out of balance, the moves round the roof eventually relent to good jams and a resting place. Above, the true line of the crack is followed to the top, with a couple of awkward moves. It is possible to sneak off to the left here but this is definitely cheating. The first part of Great Crack contains some sustained and tiring finger jamming, particularly round the bulge, and the tempting slot may not be quite as useful as first hoped. The steepness only gradually relents to a wider section of crack as it nears the top.

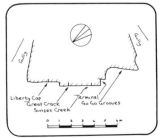

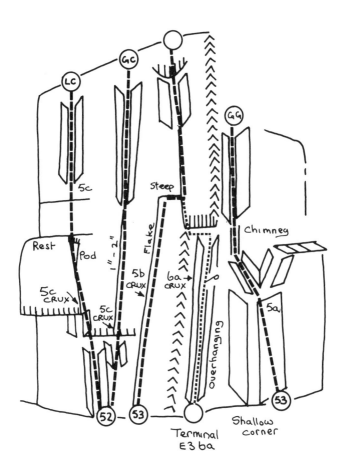

53: SUNSET CREEK & GO GO GROOVES (E1, HVS) 19m, 20m

Summary: Two more quality routes from the Upper Tor stable. Sunset Creek, the right-hand route on the front of the buttress, is a slightly easier version of Great Crack, a bit less steep and with better holds, but still a tough little cookie. Go Go Grooves has a different character, wandering in and out of a crack and groove system at the right end of the crag.

Best Conditions: Both routes dry fairly rapidly, although in summer the trees tend to shade the lower part of the crag.

Approach: Important. Approach via Willersley Castle. *See* Approaches for Upper Tor under Wildcat Crags.

First Ascents: Sunset Creek – Doug Scott and Steve Read in July 1963 using 3 points of aid and freed before 1981. Go Go Grooves – Doug Scott and Bill Cheverst in July 1963.

Starting Points: Sunset Creek – below the righthand crack. Go Go Grooves – at the wall 3m right of the corner at the right end of the crag.

Descent: Walk back through the jungle and down to the right.

Sunset Creek is probably the most popular route on Upper Tor. It is highly protectable and, although steep and sustained at its grade, it is possible to get a hands-off rest just below the small leaning headwall. For those finding things too easy, try the crack which runs up the right arête of the buttress to join Sunset Creek at the end of the traverse right. This is Terminal (E2 5c).

Go Go Grooves is a less demanding route than its companions, but none the less enjoyable, wending its way up pleasant cracks and grooves.

WILLERSLEY CASTLE ROCKS

Willersley Castle Rocks form a 40m high, 300m long, north-facing escarpment overlooking the River Derwent and a footpath which links the A6 at Cromford to the church on Station Road. The rock is generally excellent, but the screen of trees combined with the northerly aspect of the crag means that it can remain damp and gloomy for some time after a wet spell. The crag is very popular and contains many excellent middle-grade routes.

Approaches: **Please read this section.** As with parts of Wildcat Crags, the access situation to Willersley Castle Rocks is delicate. The crags and the surrounding land are owned by Methodist Guild Holidays and climbers are all too obvious from the Castle which is used as a holiday home. The path below the crag is used by holiday makers and family parties, so please contain your language, particularly the blasphemous oaths, and keep the volume down. Offence has already been caused and selfish or thoughtless behaviour risks a total ban of climbing on the crag.

   Do not park by the gate on the A6 as the police seem to take exception to this. From Matlock Bath, continue past the gate and the junction to Cromford, and turn left down Station Road, past Arkwright's Mill, to a car-park on the right by the canal. Walk down the road, turn left onto the footpath by the church which leads back to the crag. Parking is also possible in Cromford village.

   Routes are described from left to right.

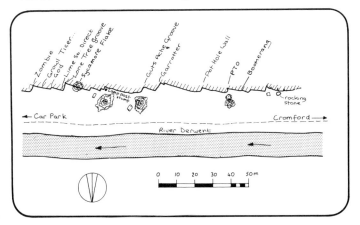

54: ZOMBIE & GROWL TIGER'S LAST STAND (E2, E2) 25m, 20m

Summary: Two powerful little routes in fine positions. Zombie takes a fierce leaning crack, which springs from part way up Great Corner and requires a determined approach. Growl Tiger climbs the unlikely-looking block roof to its right. Both routes can be well protected, Zombie particularly so.

First Ascents: Zombie – Steve Read and S. Hunt in 1957 as an aid route, and freed by Keith Myhill in 1970. Growl Tiger's Last Stand – Martin Taylor and Pete Brayshaw in June 1976.

Best Conditions: Dries fairly quickly for Willersley. *See* introductory notes to Willersley Castle Rocks.

Approach: *See* Approaches under Willersley Castle Rocks.

Starting Points: Zombie – at the highly polished line of pockets to the right of Great Corner. Growl Tiger – at the left-slanting groove, 7m right of Great Corner.

Descent: Both routes finish on a ledge with an abseil chain.

Zombie starts up a line of polished pockets which are usually desperate, particularly with slightly damp boots. Above, the crack rapidly steepens and there are awkward moves crossing some small overlaps where the left rib of the crack pushes you out of balance. Protection is excellent but, once committed to the climbing, the next hands-off rest is the belay ledge.

   Despite the block roof, Growl Tiger's Last Stand responds better to good technique than thuggery. There is a peg below the roof for protection but, once established on the lip, it is deceptively difficult to remain there and fix protection. However, there are some good small wires above the roof and it is worth having these ready to hand.

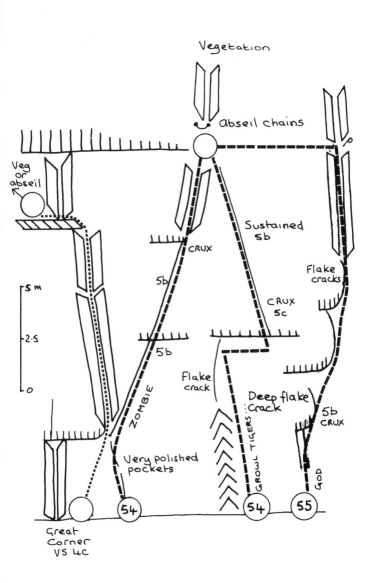

Vegetation

Abseil chains

Veg or abseil

Sustained 5b

CRUX

5b

CRUX 5c

Flake cracks

5b

Flake crack

Deep flake Crack

5b CRUX

Very polished pockets

ZOMBIE

GROWL TIGERS

GOD

5 m

2·5

0

Great Corner VS 4C

54

54

55

55: GOD & LIME STREET DIRECT (E1, E1) 25m, 40m

Summary: Two contrasting routes: God is steep and vindictive, particularly in its lower section, Lime Street Direct involves fine technical climbing up the thin groove. Protection is good on both routes. One or two larger devices may be useful for the start of God.

First Ascents: God – Steve Read and S. Hunt in 1957 as an aid route, and freed by Ted Wells and Norman Lees in 1968. Lime Street Direct – Steve Read and S. Hunt as an aid route, and freed by Ted Wells and Brian (Henry) Palmer in 1968.

Best Conditions: Dries fairly quickly for Willersley. *See* introductory notes to Willersley Castle Rocks.

Approach: *See* Approaches under Willersley Castle Rocks.

Starting Point: God may move in mysterious ways but most climbers start at the bulging flake right of Growl Tiger. *See* topo on previous page. Lime Street Direct starts at a slim groove in the arête further to the right. A difficult variation start (6a) is the Superdirect thin cracks below the main groove.

Descent: God – avoid divine retribution by traversing left to the abseil chains on Zombie. Lime Street Direct – traverse left (facing in) to the descent path.

God was probably meant as an expletive rather than as a form of adoration by the authors of the route. The start overhangs horribly and it is possible to become jammed in the tapering slot. A thuggish approach will usually resolve matters here and once you have swung out above the slot it is possible to obtain a semi-breather. Above, a groove continues in fine position until it is possible to escape left to the stance of Zombie.

Lime Street Direct is one of the most popular routes on Willersley, hence the rather polished state of the rock. Despite this, the route is very worth while, requiring delicate footwork and some slightly scary moves to gain the groove, which is then taken by excellent bridging and jamming. Mountaineers will delight in the fact that, unlike the companion routes, this climb reaches the summit.

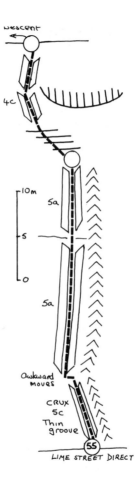

Descent

4c

10m

5

0

5a

5a

awkward
moves

CRUX
5c
Thin
groove

55

LIME STREET DIRECT

56: LONE TREE GROOVE & SYCAMORE FLAKE (HVS, VS) 40m, 50m

Summary: Two splendid lines and popular routes up the prominent, right-facing corners right of Lime Street Direct (55). The crux of Lone Tree is the steep start which is adequately protected.

First Ascent: Lone Tree Groove – Doug Scott and Steve Read in 1964. Sycamore Flake (originally called Hankering) – Steve Read and H. Harrison in 1959.

Best Conditions: The lower reaches of both routes can remain desperately damp and slippery even after many other routes have dried out.

Approach: *See* Approaches under Willersley Castle Rocks.

Starting Point: Lone Tree Groove – below the prominent corner, right of the arête of Lime Street Direct. Sycamore Flake – to the right of the corner, at an obvious right to left flake containing a sycamore tree.

Descent: Gain the path along the top of the crag, turn left and follow this to a scramble descent or alternatively, abseil from one of the many trees.

The crux of Lone Tree Groove arrives at the bulge where a bunch of tat can sometimes be found. A few strenuous moves takes you to a lone tree, after which it becomes a little easier. The stance is shared with Lime Street Direct (55) and from here the climbing is less demanding, though a little suspect in places before the solid final groove is reached.

   Sycamore Flake gives some good climbing until the groove reaches the grassy terrace where things degenerate a little and an exit has to be found by wandering up and to the right.

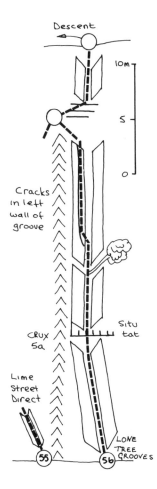

Descent

10m

5

0

Cracks
in left
wall of
groove

Situ
tat

CRUX
5a

Lime
Street
Direct

LONE
TREE
GROOVES

55

5b

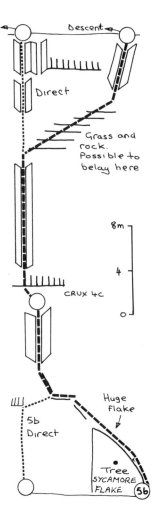

Descent

Direct

Grass and
rock.
Possible to
belay here

8m

4

0

CRUX 4c

5b
Direct

Huge
Flake

Tree
SYCAMORE
FLAKE

5b

57: GUTS ACHE GROOVE & GARROTTER (VS, VS) 35m, 35m

Summary: Two enjoyable routes with fine groove climbing. Both routes can be well protected. Garrotter is particularly popular and becoming a little polished.

First Ascents: Guts Ache Groove – Steve Read and K. Beech in 1959 using aid. Aid was whittled down to 1 point by Des Hadlum and B. Turner later that year. Garrotter – Steve Read and K. Beech in 1959.

Best Conditions: The upper grooves of both routes can be a little slow to dry after a wet spell because of the surrounding greenery.

Approach: *See* Approaches under Willersley Castle Rocks.

Starting Point: Guts Ache Groove – behind the prominent tree with the Y-shaped trunk, below a left-to-right slanting groove. Garrotter – below the slabby groove containing a small horizontal tree, to the right of Guts Ache Groove.

Descent: Abseil from one of the many trees along the top of the crag or walk to the right along the ridge to a descent path on the left, which traverses the west end of the crag just above the main road.

Two very popular excursions, unfortunately reflected in the shiny holds. Good protection can usually be arranged on the routes but a little care is required on Garrotter, which weaves in and out of the slabby overhangs.

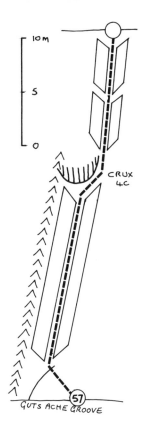

CRUX
4C

GUTS ACHE GROOVE

57

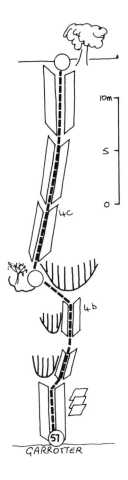

4C

4b

GARROTTER

57

58: POTHOLE WALL & GANGUE
GROOVES (VS, HVS) 35m, 45m

Summary: Two superb and varied routes weaving around the complex area of rock below the bulging headwall. For the most part the rock is good and the routes well protected.

First Ascents: Pothole Wall – Steve Read and B. Jackson in 1959, using aid. Gangue Grooves – Doug Scott and Steve Read in 1964, using some aid. The first free ascent is not recorded.

Best Conditions: Both routes dry relatively quickly, although the upper sections may retain some dampness.

Approach: *See* Approaches under Willersley Castle Rocks.

Starting Points: Pothole Wall – at a shallow, right-facing corner just right of the large ivy-coated tree. Gangue Grooves – to the right of Pothole Wall, below an area of black rock containing a thin, discontinuous crack.

Descent: Abseil from one of the many trees along the top of the crag or walk right along the ridge to a descent path on the left, which traverses the west end of the crag just above the main road.

Despite the strange and suspect-looking rock, both these routes give some excellent climbing in impressive situations. Pothole Wall avoids the curious pothole by a fingery little traverse right in a very exposed position, which constitutes the crux of that route. There is usually a piece of *in situ* gear on the traverse which is best backed up.

Gangue Grooves is a route of contrasts: the lower section is on strange, 'crozzly' rock, steep but with the opportunity for some good wires, and leads on to a broad, slabby area where it is possible to belay at an old jammed wire. Despite the apparent slabbiness of the climbing, the final groove, past an old peg, probably constitutes the crux and, because of this, it is probably safer to run the two pitches out into one.

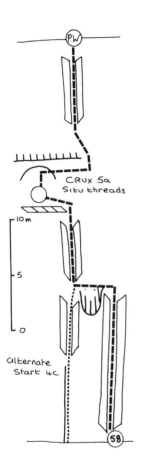

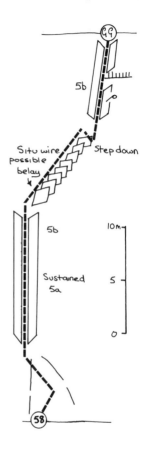

59: PTO (E2) 35m

Summary: An improbable line crossing a large roof at a reasonable grade. Protection is excellent, some of it old and *in situ* which should be treated with care. Extra clippers for the pegs and a few long extenders to avoid rope drag may be useful.

First Ascent: Steve Read in 1958 as an aid route at A2. It was subsequently reduced to 3 points by Pete Crew in 1962 and finally freed by Keith Myhill in 1969.

Best Conditions: The overhang can sometimes retain a few nasty wet bits.

Approach: *See* Approaches for Willersley Castle Rocks.

Starting Point: Below the prominent corner leading to a large roof.

Descent: Abseil from one of the many trees along the top of the crag, or walk right, along the ridge, to a descent path on the left which traverses the west end of the crag just above the main road.

One of the joys of PTO is its improbable nature. The groove is straightforward but the huge roof persistently attempts to intimidate anyone who approaches. On closer inspection, it is not too bad and there are a few items of antique iron ware for starters. Once attacked, superb jugs come to hand and it is possible to become over confident, as you swing from the lip of the overhang, below an easy-looking groove. However, it is not quite all over as leaving the jug and entering the groove constitutes the crux and has been the site of some amusing contortions prior to an embarrassing sag on to a peg.

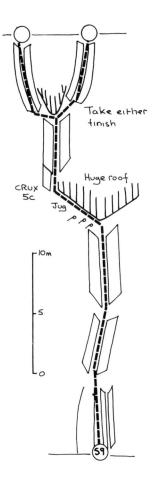

Take either finish

Huge roof

CRUX
5c

Jug

10m

5

0

59

60: BOOMERANG (HVS) 38m

Summary: A well-polished but enjoyable route taking a series of slabby corners separated by overlaps. The route contains a sprinkling of ancient pegs but natural protection is also available.

First Ascent: Steve Read and S. Hunt in 1960, using 3 points of aid, and subsequently free climbed by Pete Crew.

Best Conditions: Not a good idea in damp conditions.

Approach: *See* Approaches for Willersley Castle Rocks. Boomerang is at the right-hand end of the crag, a few metres right of the start of PTO.

Starting Point: At a slabby wall below a series of rightward-leading overlaps and grooves.

Descent: Descend the back of the crag and traverse right just above the main road.

Awkward moves around the overlap are not helped by the polish on the holds. A selection of old pegs and good wire placements usually make this a safe and sometimes exciting ascent. The name probably refers to the habit of aspiring leaders ending up close to where they started off.

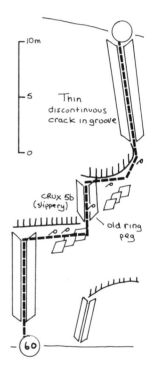

Thin discontinuous crack in groove

CRUX 5b (slippery)

old ring peg

Dovedale Area

The climbing in Dovedale is concentrated in a beautiful and popular 4km stretch of valley between the cottages at Milldale in the north and the stepping stones below Thorpe Cloud in the south. Much of the climbing in Dovedale is steep and exhilarating, set on isolated tors and pinnacles above the river. The harder routes tend to be fingery and descents from the various pinnacles are often Dolomitic in character. A wonderland of rock.

Approaches: Dovedale can be approached from either Thorpe village or Milldale. Both ends are easily accessible by car from the A515 Buxton to Ashbourne road. There is limited parking just beyond Milldale, and a large car-park at the south end of Dovedale below Thorpe Cloud (a pointed hill) at SK 147509. Dovedale is not easily reached without private transport. The Buxton to Ashbourne bus route along the A515 is probably the closest approach. The routes on Tissington Spires are best approached from the Thorpe Cloud end of the Dale; Ravens Tor, Ilam Rock and Pickering Tors are best approached from Milldale.

Accommodation: Camping – at Alstonfield and, in the summer, some local farmers let out their fields.
Youth hostels – at Ilam Hall, near Ilam village, at SK 131506 and at Hartington Village to the north.
B. & b. – available at many of the local pubs, farms and villages.
Bivouacs – Dove Holes cave may provide some rather sloping shelter. The best cave is on Dovedale Castle at SK 148515, above the river on the Staffordshire bank at the south end of the valley.

Services: The nearest town is Ashbourne, some 4km along the A515 past the junction for Thorpe. Thorpe, Alstonfield and Hartington have post offices. The closest shops are probably in Ashbourne. Refreshments are usually available in Milldale and sometimes at Thorpe Cloud car-park and there are toilets at Milldale, Thorpe and Thorpe Cloud car-park. Pubs can be found in Alstonfield, at the top of Milldale, and in Thorpe village. The Jug and Glass, 1.5km north of the Hartington turn off, is usually well worth a visit. Petrol is obtainable in Hartington, Thorpe and at Newhaven on the A515. There is a Mountain Rescue Post at Ilam Hall in Ilam.

A Concise History: According to legend, the first ascent of a climb in Dovedale occurred in 1903 with Samuel Turner's top rope ascent of Ilam Rock. History does not say how many points of aid were used but he is recorded as completing a head stand on the summit; re-enactments are not recommended. A more conventional ascent of this famous landmark had to wait a further eleven years. Up to 1914, sporadic visits were made to Dovedale by several climbers including J. W. Putrell, Henry Bishop and Eric Byne. Siegfried Herford and A. R. Thompson's ascent of the horrible Original Route on Pickering Pinnacle must rank as an outstanding act of boldness. However, one does wonder whether perhaps having got committed they could not get back!

Real development in Dovedale did not start until the 1950s when Joe Brown and members of the Rock and Ice started to invade the valley. Means of protection were poor and pitons were used with fairly free abandon. A list of activists from those days includes many famous names, Joe Brown, Nat Allen, Slim Sorrell, George Band, Don Whillans, John Sumner and Roy Leeming. Routes included Scuthern Rib, Venery, Brown's Blunder (Raven Tor), The Groove, The White Edge (aid) and The Wong Edge on Ilam Rock, and Left Hand Route (aid) on Raven Tor. The White Edge and Left Hand Route were both climbed with aid but were real achievements none the less. Eventually free ascents started to dominate the scene and the free climbing potential of the valley began to be recognized. The publication of Graham West's *Rock Climbs on the Mountain Limestone of Derbyshire* in 1961 soon brought Dovedale into the open.

During the next ten years, many of the modern classics were discovered: Pete Williams and John Amies climbed John Peel and Snakes Alive; Roy Leeming, Thunderball and Anaconda; Nat Allen, Watchblock Direct and Simeon, and Bob Hassall and John Critchlow, The Claw and Bill Baley. The end of the 1960s was marked by Jack Street's ascent of the superb Adjudicator Wall, a climb which remained unrepeated for several years. Development progressed sporadically until the arrival of John Codling and Chris Calow in 1977. These two were to be prolific activists during the next few years, generating a plethora of fine routes, including Ten Craters of Wisdom and the splendid Tales of The Riverbank (E4 6a) with 1 aid point. During 1982, Dovedale Church, along with many other crags, received a good deal of attention, with the Lee brothers, Dominic and Daniel, being at the forefront of the development with such routes as their desperate Jungle Land and Amazonia. As the climbing scene expanded, more and more climbers became active in the Dale. Especially notable was Ron Fawcett's impressive ascent of Eye of The Tiger (E6 6c) on the overhanging face of Ilam Rock.

Since then, many 'last great problems' have been climbed. Stars have burned bright and faded but Dovedale still remains the same great adventure.

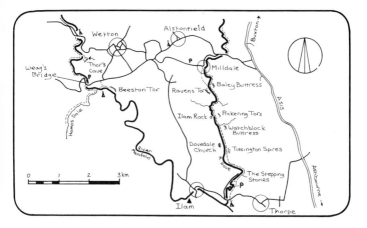

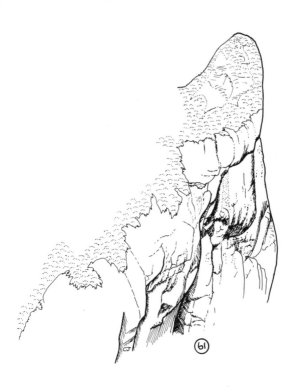

Roy Small and Les Naylor on The Claw (Route 61), Baley Buttress, Dovedale. (Photo: Chris Jackson.)

61: THE CLAW & CLAW LEFT HAND
(HVS, HVS) 41m, 42m

Summary: Two steep routes in nail-biting position, joining for a common finish which spirals round the buttress to reach the top.

First Ascents: The Claw – A. Critchlow and Rob Hassall in 1966 with one aid point, and later freed by Jack Street, who added Claw Left Hand.

Best Conditions: Claw Left Hand may retain a little dampness in its deeper recesses but the buttress faces west and dries quite quickly.

Approach: From Milldale follow the footpath downstream for about 600m to a wall and stile. Baley Buttress lies up the slope to the left.

Starting Points: Claw Left Hand – at the obvious slot chimney near the toe of the buttress. The Claw – 2m to the right of the chimney.

Descent: Traverse left (facing uphill) to steep grass and scree.

Despite their similar grades, The Claw is usually found to be much less of a struggle. The smooth water-washed groove of Claw Left Hand has a distinct tendency to fight back and any lack of friction due to dampness soon pushes the grade up towards 5c. Exiting the slot is awkward but above this the two routes combine and enter an exciting little overhanging chimney which leads to the stance. It is possible to escape but that will mean missing out on a delectable pitch, the route now follows a helter skelter fault line round the buttress to reach a notch below a satisfyingly sharp summit. Pure Dovedale.

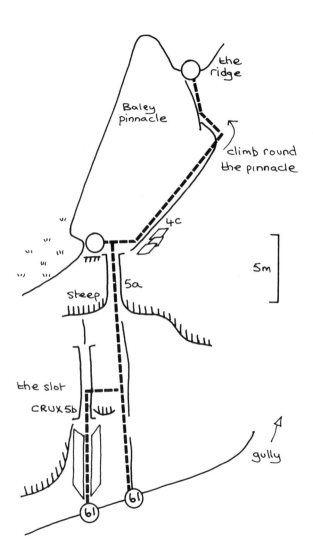

the ridge

Baley pinnacle

climb round the pinnacle

4c

5m

steep

5a

the slot

CRUX 5b

gully

61   61

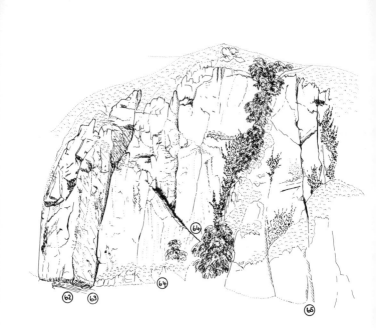

62: SOUTHERN RIB (HVS) 49m

Summary: Everybody's favourite, a justifiably popular classic following an unlikely-looking line at a reasonable grade. The position is always excellent and protection more than adequate.

First Ascent: Joe Brown and George Band at some time between 1952 and 1954 as an A2 aid route. It was freed by Roy Leeming in 1965.

Best Conditions: Unfortunately, Raven Tor faces east and only gets the early morning sun. This can be idyllic on a warm summer's day but unpleasantly cold and draughty off season. It dries a little slowly after prolonged rain.

Approach: Opposite Baley Buttress, from Milldale, follow the path downstream for 600m to the wall. Paddle across the river at one of the many weirs and ascend the grassy bank to the foot of the crag. For those with hydrophobia, or in times of flood, it is possible to reach the crag by an alternate route from Milldale: follow the alley at the side of the toilets, turn left, and climb through woods and fields for 500m until it is possible to walk down to the foot of the crag.

Starting Point: At the left end of the crag, below a steep wall with a disappearing flake leading to a ledge at 15m.

Descent: From the grassy slopes at the top of the crag, head back and right to a wall, follow this, bearing right, to a steep descent by a rickety wire fence.

A 'must' for any visiting party to Ravens Tor, giving all the excitement of limestone climbing in impressive situations. The initial wall is steep and was originally a little shaky but its popularity has ensured that most, though not all, of the looseness has now gone. There is a steep move just below the belay ledge but it is possible to arrange some solid protection before commitment. The second pitch launches out into an intricate series of hanging grooves. The first moves are a little intimidating as the grooves hang over the steep wall taken by The Temptress (E5 6a), but there is always good protection and a jug when it is needed. The line of the route is somewhat convoluted here and it is possible to suffer some considerable rope drag unless care is taken with the runnering. Above all difficulties, but still in fine position, the route traverses right to a cosy little stance below the last easier pitch which gradually fades into steep grass. Belays can be found well back from the top of the route.

63: LEFT HAND ROUTE (E1) 39m

Summary: A superb and strenuous pitch up the obvious groove at the left side of the main face.

First Ascent: Like many of the Dovedale routes, this fine line was first climbed as an aid route, by John Sumner and B. Knox at some time in the 1950s. It was freed by Jack Street and Geoff Birtles in 1967.

Best Conditions: The route can take a little drainage. *See* Best Conditions for Route 62.

Approach: As for Route 62.

Starting Point: Below the obvious groove which separates the steep left-hand section of the crag from the more slabby central section.

Descent: From the grassy slopes at the top of the crag, head back and right to a wall, follow this, bearing right, to a steep descent by a rickety wire fence.

Jack Street was a powerful and athletic climber and was probably the best of the notorious Stoney Middleton Cioch Club. He was to be the author of several fine climbs in Dovedale during the late 1960s. This was one of his early offerings.

The route progressively steepens as the main crack is approached and, although it takes some wonderful protection, the problem is in hanging on to place it. Beyond the *in situ* peg, the rock bulges but the left wall of the groove develops and it is possible to get 'spragged out' into a bridging position which takes a little of the strain off the arms. Things do not really ease though until the first ledge is reached just below the belay and many an aspirant Extreme leader has found himself sagging from a runner placed with his last ounces of strength left. However, at the stance it is possible to extend your belay so that you can see your second having a bad time. Easier corners lead to the grassy top. A decent belay can usually be found well back at a small outcrop.

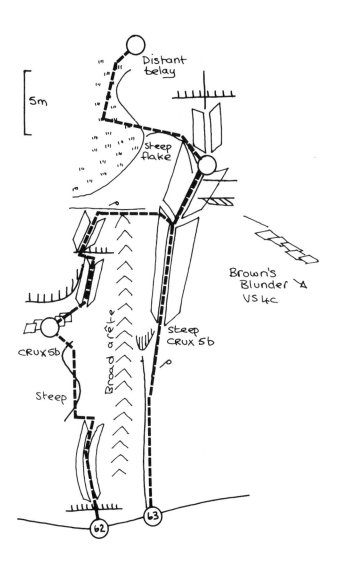

Distant
belay

5m

steep
flake

Brown's
Blunder ▲
VS 4c

steep
CRUX 5b

Broad arête

CRUX 5b

Steep

62   63

64: AQUARIUS & CENTRAL WALL
(E1, E2) 30m, 33m

Summary: Two fine test-pieces up the steep wall above the ramp line of Brown's Blunder. Aquarius has a bold and committing start; Central Wall is steep and fingery with a well protected crux below a bulge near the top of pitch 1. For those finding things a little tame, there are three alternative eliminate finishes to Central Wall. A few extra medium-sized wires may be found useful.

First Ascents: Aquarius – Jack Street and Tom Proctor in 1968. Central Wall – Tom Proctor and Keith Myhill in April 1969, using 1 point of aid. This was an impressive, nearly free ascent of the old aid route Lewd Wall, which was first climbed by R. Leeming in the 1950s.

Best Conditions: Of the routes on Raven Tor, these routes probably dry most quickly.

Approach: As for Route 62.

Starting Point: Both routes start from the ascending right-to-left ramp line of Brown's Blunder. Central Wall starts a little way up the ramp, 6m left of Central Gully. Aquarius starts 6m further up the ramp at a thread below a steep pillar, although many choose to add a lower pitch below the ramp, which actually belongs to The Raven (E2 5c).

Descent: From the grassy slopes at the top of the crag, head back and right to a wall, follow this rightwards to a steep descent by a rickety wire fence.

Two good examples of steep crack climbing on limestone. Aquarius can seem scary as the first moves from the ramp overhang somewhat and it is not easy to stop and fix runners. Things soon relent a little and good holds and runner placements soon arrive. The rest of the route is pure pleasure up easier cracks to the top. Those wishing to add an introductory pitch (*see* topo) will be well rewarded with some fine crack climbing, low in the 5c category but a good introduction to the style of Central Wall.

Central Wall gives a taste of the harder crack climbing problems to be found on limestone, but it is well protected and in splendid position. The author Tom Proctor went on to put up some of the hardest routes on Peak limestone during the early 1970s. Most of the difficulties of the route are from finger jamming up the steepening crack. Runners abound but it is easy to fill up the finger placements and make things really hard. Above the belay on pitch 2, the route moves off left into some steep territory but it is easier than it looks. Three alternative finishes are available, which should keep you busy: The Doldrums (E3 6a), Judas (E5 6b) and the direct finish (E 4bb).

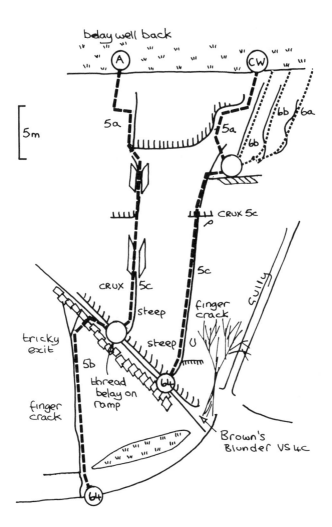

belay well back

5m

A CW

5a 5a

bb 6a

bb

CRUX 5c

5c

CRUX 5c

steep

finger crack

steep U

Gully

tricky exit

5b

thread belay on ramp

finger crack

Brown's Blunder VS 4c

65: VENERY & PARROT FACE (HVS, HVS) 45m, 40m

Summary: Two steep jamming cracks on the exposed upper wall at the right end of the crag. Both routes will take some large protection.

First Ascents: Venery – Joe Brown, at some time in the 1950s, using several wooden wedges for aid, and free climbed by Harry Smith in 1963. Parrot Face – Jack Street in 1966.

Best Conditions: The first pitch can retain a little dampness from the surrounding vegetation. The cracks generally dry quite quickly.

Approach: As for Route 62.

Starting Point: At the foot of the buttress right of Central Gully at a large flake. Parrot Face takes the upper right-hand crack and Venery, the left crack.

Descent: Walk back and right to a descent by the rickety fence.

Two worthwhile routes giving some good practice in hand jamming up steep rock. The little roof at the top of Parrot Face probably constitutes the hardest part of the routes.

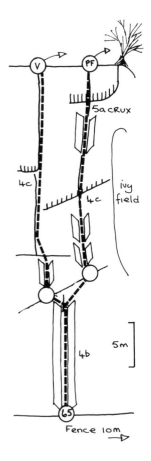

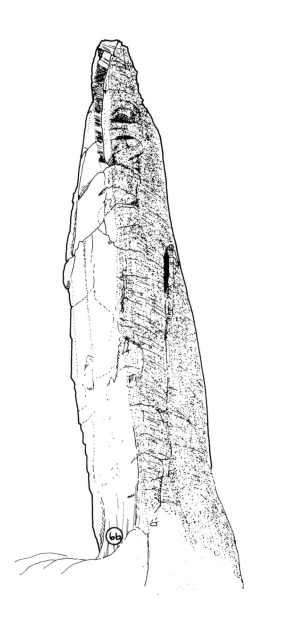

66

66: EASTER ISLAND & WHITE EDGE (E1, E3) 28m

Summary: Steep, spectacular climbing up the riverside arête of Dovedale's most famous pinnacle, Ilam Rock. The Easter Island start and The White Edge finish gives a superb combination at E2.

First Ascent: The White Edge – Joe Brown and Ron Moseley, possibly in 1953, as an A2 aid route. The initial peg-scarred crack deterred most would-be free ascensionists and it was not until Ron Fawcett's ascent in 1978 that the original line succumbed. Easter Island – Ed Ward-Drummond and H. Green-Armytage in 1972. A milestone in climbing in Dovedale.

Best Conditions: The routes can be cold and exposed in the winter months. Both routes dry quickly.

Approach: *See* the plan of Pickering Tor on page 173. The 30m pinnacle of Ilam Rock is not easily missed, springing straight from the river bank opposite the footpath, some 1km downstream of Milldale. A footbridge over the river gives access to the routes. From Thorpe Cloud the approach is a little longer.

Starting Point: At the river end of a ledge below the overhanging, downstream side of the pinnacle. Some sort of belay may be advisable.

Descent: By abseil only, from slings and things down the shorter, upstream side of the pinnacle.

A must for any competent visiting party and those wishing to become a tourist attraction. Ward-Drummond's controversial ascent of Ilam Rock marked the start of route renaming. Drummond mistakenly claimed to have free climbed The White Edge but, although there was some common rock, the lines were not the same. In the early 1970s route names were almost sacrosanct, The White Edge particularly so, being a Joe Brown Classic, and this attempt at route changing caused much reaction. Happily both routes now exist side by side.

The start of The White Edge takes a line of excruciating peg holes up a thin crack which joins the arête a few metres up. This has never proved to be a popular start and it is far more enjoyable (not to say easier) to follow the arête as for Easter Island and then take to The White Edge around the arête on the overhanging downstream face of Ilam Rock. Once established round the arête, things are very steep and exposed and a couple of powerful moves are required to reach easier going. However, protection is excellent, the holds positive and within a couple of metres a small corner is reached. The final easy bulge has seen a few wobblers.

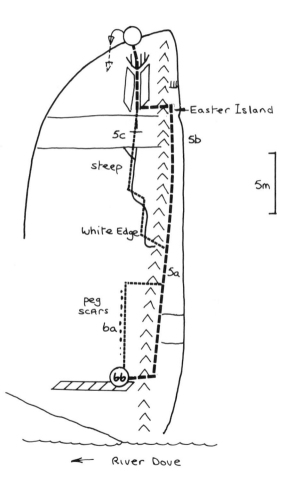

Easter Island

5c

5b

steep

White Edge

5a

peg
scars

ba

6b

5m

← River Dove

67: PICKERING'S OVERHANG & THE FLAKE (E1, E1) 21m

Summary: Two good exposed climbs arriving at the summit of the long, narrow ridge almost opposite Ilam Rock. Protection on both is excellent and from the narrow summit the views are remarkable.

First Ascent: Pickering's Overhang – Joe Brown and Don Whillans, probably in 1953, and graded VS and A1. The first free ascent is not recorded but the route was free by the early 1970s. The Flake (originally called Pickering Flake) – Jack Street, Paul Nunn and Rod Haslam in August 1969.

Best Conditions: At almost any time as the routes face south and take little drainage.

Approach: As for Route 66, but continue past the footbridge, close to the pinnacle of Ilam Rock, and ascend the left side of a long ridge, with a cave at its foot, to a comfortable saddle. This is Pickering Pinnacle.

Starting Point: A little below the saddle, on the downstream side of the pinnacle is an obvious groove and overhang. Start at belays below this for Pickering's Overhang, just to the right for The Flake.

Descent: By abseil. There are two rusty pegs joined by tapes below the uphill end of the pinnacle which allow a short abseil to the saddle. These also serve as the belay.

Pickering's Overhang soon steepens and the crux is not passing the overhang but rather progressing up the wall above. Odd bits of tat usually make the moves feel safer but those who dally may find their fingers uncurling from the holds and curling round the runners. The crest of the pinnacle is so narrow that it is possible to sit astride it. The Flake only seems to succumb to thuggery and strong fingers and, although the route can be well protected, success is only achieved after some strenuous laybacking and finger jamming. It is harder than it looks.

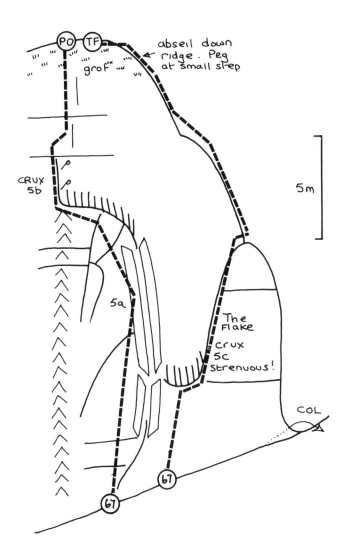

absell down
ridge. Peg
at small step

grof

CRUX
5b

5m

5a

The
Flake

crux
5c
strenuous!

COL

67

67

68: ADJUDICATOR WALL (E3) 39m

Summary: A tremendous route, technical and sustained, on excellent rock and with ample protection. The most sought after E3 in the valley.

First Ascent: Jack Street and Geoff Birtles in May 1969, using 1 point of aid to gain the final groove.

Best Conditions: The route catches a good deal of available sun but takes some drainage after prolonged rain.

Approach: Watchblock Buttress is not easily seen from the path, but can be recognized by a precariously balanced block on its summit. Legend has it that if you watch the block for long enough you will see it move, hence the name. The buttress can be approached from Milldale or Thorpe Cloud; it is about equidistant from both. From Milldale walk downstream, past Ilam Rock, to a prominent, rounded buttress at the side of the path, which is Lion Rock. Take the scree gully just downstream of this. If you find yourself at the boardwalks you are some 200m too far downstream. From Thorpe Cloud walk upstream, along a boardwalk, and take the scree gully on the right just before Lion Rock. Watchblock Buttress is characterized by a cave arch at its left end.

Starting Point: Start on the right, at the toe of the buttress.

Descent: By abseil from the tree at the top of the route. For those trained in jungle warfare it is just possible to fight your way back and left into a descent gully.

A wonderfully sustained pitch with protection just where it is needed. The start of the route is shared with the E1, Nancy Whisky, which climbs the thin groove leading to the upper slabs. Most leaders choose to place some protection a little way up this to protect the first set of hard moves across the traverse, the height of the runner up this route being in some way related to the state of intimidation. The holds are now becoming a little polished and an extended reach left to the jug on this and the next awkward section of traverse may be found to be a safer solution to the problem than the use of 'technique' on smooth holds. The crux comes at the peg that was originally used for aid. It is placed in a thin crack which provides only a mediocre finger hold and the footholds across this section are generally conspicuous by their absence. Once the technical difficulties are passed, better holds arrive but the climbing continues steeply for several more moves and many a party has successfully negotiated the crux only to slump onto a runner in the final crack.

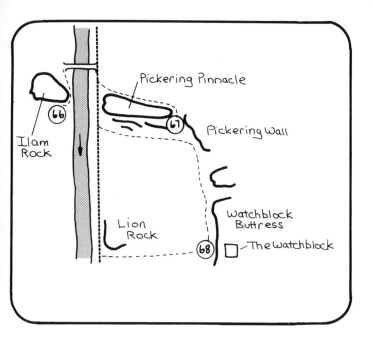

Ilam Rock

66

Pickering Pinnacle

67

Pickering Wall

Lion Rock

Watchblock Buttress

68 □ The Watchblock

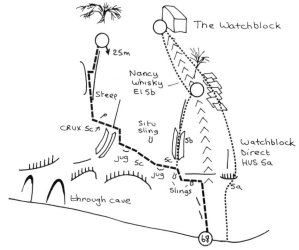

The Watchblock

25m

Steep

CRUX Sc ↗

Situ sling ∪

Nancy whisky E1 5b

5b

5c

Jug 5c

Jug

Slings

Watchblock Direct HVS 5a

5a

through cave

68

TISSINGTON SPIRES

Tissington Spires form an intricate series of pinnacles and ridges above the River Dove, some 1km downstream of Ilam Rock. The Spires offer some superb climbing in tremendous position but, because of their complexity, climbs can sometimes be difficult to locate. Recent controversial tree clearing by the National Trust has helped in this respect.

Approaches: The closest approach to Tissington Spires is from the National Trust car-park at Thorpe Cloud. From the car-park, follow the path upstream crossing to the true left bank at the stepping stones. Follow the path, over a rise (Lover's Leap) and down to a stile. Tissington Spires is on the right. About 100m upstream of the stile, a well-marked path leads up to a cave beside fencing and then left into South Gully.
   From Milldale, follow the path downstream, past Dove Holes and Ilam Rock, along the board walks, past Raynard's Cave to a ruined pump-house on the left of the path. This is about 1km below Ilam Rock. Downstream from the pump-house, on the left, are the three approach gullies to the climbing on Tissington Spires.
   Across the river, accessible by wading one of the weirs, is the imposing pinnacle of Dovedale Church, which is actually four pinnacles paired by two archways.

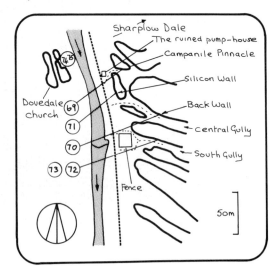

Bob Conway on Adjudicator Wall (Route 68), Watchblock Buttress, Dovedale. (Photo: Chris Jackson.)

69: WHACKO & THE MAN WITH X-RAY EYES (E3, E1) 25m

Summary: Steep and pumpy climbing on Campanile Pinnacle – the most upstream of the Tissington Spires. Both routes require a positive attitude. Protection is generally good.

First Ascents: Whacko – Roy Leeming and Steve Read at some time in the 1950s, as an aid route, and freed by Martin Taylor in 1976. The Man With X-Ray Eyes – Gary and Phil Gibson in 1983.

Best Conditions: The routes start from the shady side of the pinnacle, and it can be cool and draughty at times. Being on a pinnacle, both routes dry fairly quickly.

Approach: *See* Approaches under Tissington Spires and the diagram on page 176. Campanile Pinnacle is just above the ruined pump-house. Scramble up the scree and under the south-east face of the pinnacle to a small col. The routes are on the south-east-facing wall, characterized by the arching line of Whacko.

Starting Point: Whacko – from ledges at the left side of the face, below an arching flake line. The Man With X-Ray Eyes – in a corner on the right-hand arête of the face.

Descent: By abseil only, from a tree to the col at the top of the scree.

The crux of The Man With X-Ray Eyes is in the first 10m. The start is nervy, with a good wire followed by a disgusting peg. A couple more moves and there is some dubious *in situ* gear and better wires. Above, the rock bulges horribly and further progress looks unlikely. Keep with it, amazing holds soon follow, leading to easier ground and a fine, sharp summit.

Whacko is made of sterner stuff, the curving flake line becomes progressively harder and leaves you hanging from undercuts, faced by a daunting overlap. A long reach up and right gains a good flake but those with a normal reach may be forced to lunge. Protection is good and there are numerous placements for camming devices and medium-sized wires in the curving flake.

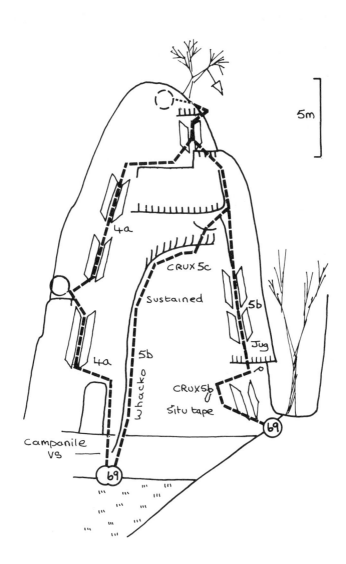

5m

4a

CRUX 5c

Sustained

5b

Jug

Whacko

5b

CRUX 5b
Situ tape

4a

Campanile
VS

69

69

70: TEN CRATERS OF WISDOM & SIMEON (VS, VS) 33m, 33m

Summary: Two popular routes on Simeon Wall with some amazing holds. The rock is excellent and protection generally good.

First Ascent: Ten Craters of Wisdom – Chris Calow (solo) in 1978. Simeon – J. R. (Nat) Allen and Derek Carnell in 1965, using 1 point of aid.

Best Conditions: The routes receive a good deal of available sun but can suffer from wet streaks after rain.

Approach: *See* Approaches under Tissington Spires. Ten Craters and Simeon are on Back Wall, an ill-named feature since it is actually the side of a long ridge. At 45m downstream of the ruined pump-house, take the scree slopes, bearing slightly right, to a narrow col which leads on to Back Wall.

Starting Point: Start below a cleaned wall leading to a ledge and Ash tree.

Descent: Walk uphill along the side of the broad ridge until it is possible to escape by easily clambering down and right into the upper part of the gully.

Two very popular routes in a delightful setting, well worth doing by any visiting party if only to experience the amazing jugs which pierce the upper slabs on Ten Craters. The crux of Simeon probably arrives at the start of pitch 2, around the cemented peg, unless one goes for the direct connection, which is a little harder. The crux on Ten Craters is on the upper wall where the rock steepens and an extended reach is required for what is obviously yet another crater. Protection can be arranged off to the right for this move.

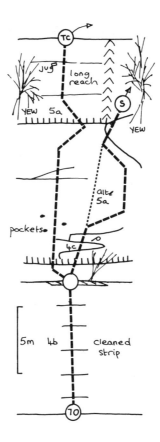

71: SILICON & MANNA MACHINE (VS, VS) 25m

Summary: Two popular and enjoyable crack climbs on yet another Dovedale pinnacle – Silicon Wall. Silicon is perhaps the better of the two.

First Ascents: Silicon – Steve Read, Roy Leeming, Derek Carnell, P. Brown and S. Hunt in 1956, by alternate leads! (according to historical records). Most of the loose rock must have fallen off on the first ascent! Manna Machine – Gary Gibson (solo) in February 1981.

Best Conditions: At almost any time. There is little drainage although the cracks may hold a little dampness.

Approach: *See* Approaches under Tissington Spires. Silicon Wall is the South face of the pinnacle nearest to the path, and just below the ruined pump-house.

Starting Point: Growing from the right edge of the pinnacle is a large ash tree. Start left of this, below slabby rocks.

Descent: Descent is by abseil or short climb (Diff) down the back (north-east) face to the col.

Pleasant climbing with some fine positions towards the top of the routes and some excellent jamming on Silicon. The section of rock on Manna Machine between the Ash tree and the foot of the upper crack is a little shattered and should be treated with care. Once at the top it is necessary to climb (about Diff) or possibly abseil down the back from the notch on the left, into the top of the gully close to the col.

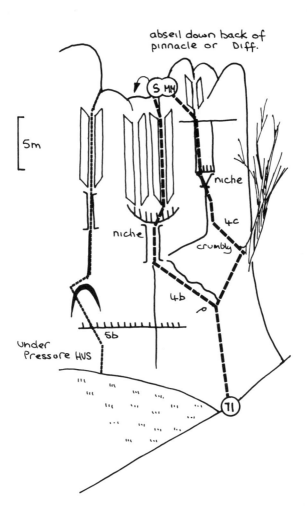

abseil down back of
pinnacle or Diff.

5 MN

5m

niche

niche

4c

crumbly

4b

p

5b

Under
Pressure HVS

TI

72: JOHN PEEL, GEORGE & YEW TREE WALL (HVS, E1, E1) 54m, 39m, 39m

Summary: *De Rigeur* for any visiting party. Three superb Dovedale classics containing some absorbing climbing on the steep pinnacle walls of South Gully.

First Ascents: John Peel – Pete (Trog) Williams and John Amies in 1964. George – Steve Read and Roy Leeming at some time in the 1950s as an aid route. This was reduced to 2 points of aid by Paul Nunn and Jeff Morgan in 1969 and freed shortly after. Yew Tree Wall – Paul Nunn and Jeff Morgan in 1969, using 1 point of aid, and freed in the early 1970s.

Best Conditions: After a wet spell the long, curving flake taken by John Peel can retain some dampness and the start of the routes can be unnervingly slippery.

Approach: Downstream of the

other pinnacles of Tissington Spires, on the left bank of the river, a path leads up to a cave and corner crack, traverses left behind a wire fence and into a large gully with an imposing left wall. This is South Gully and the wall is known as John Peel Wall.

Starting Point: John Peel – at a large ash growing close to the wall, up the gully from the start of the curving flakes. George – at a shallow groove with a tree at its base below the foot of the curving flakes. Yew Tree Wall starts further up the gully below a large yew tree at 20m, and above a tree stump.

Descent: Follow the summit ridge until it is possible to gain the head of South Gully. For John Peel and Yew Tree Wall, it is probably less hazardous to abseil from the remains of the yew tree.

In the summer months these routes, particularly John Peel, see an almost continuous stream of ascents. Once on this wall it is easy to see why; perfect rock and continuous interest combine to produce superb expeditions and the great white sheets of rock give the impression of something far higher than a modest 40m.

The technical crux of John Peel is probably the short wall just prior to gaining the corner, which forms the base of the flake. Above, it is steady progress with ample protection. The final traverse before the yew tree stump can be a little confusing as it is necessary to balance up round a bulge from one crack line to another, with no obvious markers for the right position.

George is a rather more intimidating character and the traverse out left, from the flake line of John Peel across an apparently blank wall, looks unlikely. The traverse is awkward and a little strenuous to start and appears to lead into some steep and unlikely territory. However, persistence will be rewarded with some excellent holds leading across the wall in tremendous position above the gully. Around the corner, there is a fine long groove leading to the narrow grassy summit ridge.

Yew Tree Wall contains some delectable moves between large pockets, with the crux usually well protected by *in situ* threads. Unfortunately the yew tree has suffered some irreversible damage by something or someone falling onto it and has been reduced to a sorry stump.

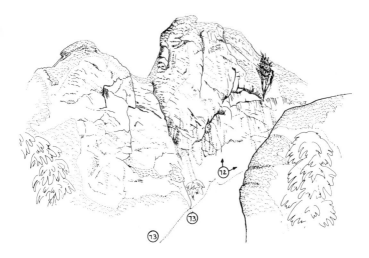

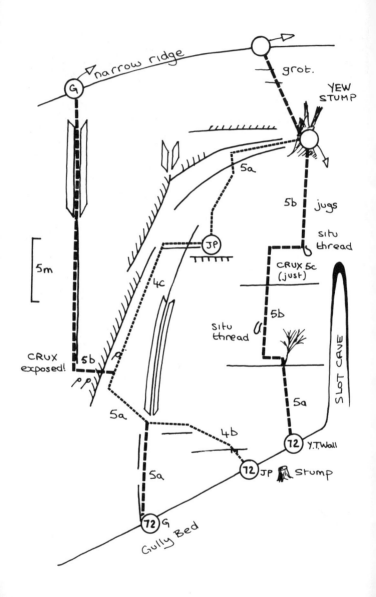

An unknown party on Ten Craters of Wisdom, Tissington Spires, Dovedale. (Photo: Chris Jackson.)

73: BRUTUS & CAESAR (HVS, E3)
30m, 45m

Summary: Brutus, in spite of the name, is a pleasant and absorbing route; Caesar, powerful and sustained for several moves is well protected and in fine position. The top pitch, although at a lower grade, maintains interest and position and lands one on the crest of the ridge of South Gully.

First Ascents: Brutus – in the 1960s, as an aid route. The first free ascent was by Pete O'Donovan and Mark Stokes in 1976. Caesar – John Codling and Chris Calow, in 1978, during the golden years of Dovedale development. The peg runner was reputedly hammered in with a large hexentric.

Best Conditions: Both routes dry fairly quickly.

Approach: Downstream of the other pinnacles of Tissington Spires, on the left bank of the river, a path leads up to a cave and corner crack, traverses left behind a wire fence and into a large gully with an imposing left wall. This is South Gully, the wall is known as John Peel Wall.

Starting Point: Brutus – below where the gully closes in, and below a crack behind a prominent sawn-off tree stump. Caesar – further up the gully, 10m below a small ledge and sapling.

Descent: Brutus – abseil back down the route from the ridge. Caesar – many parties take the descent for Brutus but the true finish leads onto the continuation ridge, from where it is possible to walk back to the top of South Gully to descend.

Although Brutus is well worth attention, Caesar is perhaps the finer route, containing some sustained and fingery moves on perfect pocketed rock – quintessential limestone climbing. The upper pitch is often ignored by parties who are just after a quick tick but it should not be too lightly dismissed. There are some exposed positions here and the pitch finishes satisfyingly on the airy crest of the ridge.

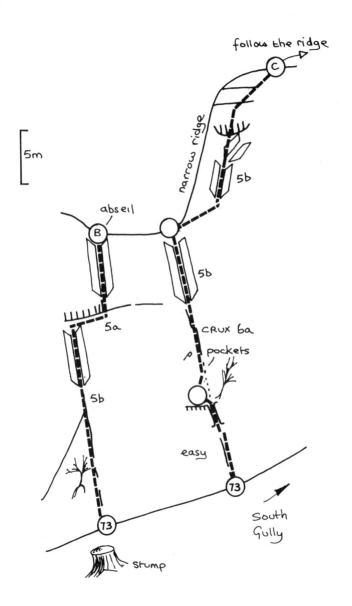

follow the ridge

C

narrow ridge

5b

abseil

B

5b

5a

5b

crux 6a

pockets

easy

73

73

South Gully

stump

5m

DOVEDALE CHURCH

Dovedale Church is the intriguing system of pinnacles on the shady Staffordshire bank of the river, opposite Tissington Spires. There are actually four pinnacles, paired by archways, forming a strange and complex arrangement of buttresses. The routes described here are all on the river face of Dovedale Church, and are mainly crack climbing in steep position.

Access is only possible by wading, usually at one of the weirs above the ruined pump-house opposite Tissington Spires. The path on the true right bank leads downstream to the stepping stones at the Thorpe Cloud end of Dovedale but should not be used for access to Dovedale Church as it is private. The pinnacles form an attractive venue for a warm summers day; the rock is excellent and protection generally good. However, as Dovedale Church is on the shady bank, it can retain some dampness after other pinnacles have dried out. Indeed, during the winter months, the pinnacles usually remain out of condition.

74: SNAKES ALIVE (VS) 24m

Summary: Technical climbing up a corner of perfect, water-washed limestone. Good protection can usually be arranged.

First Ascent: Pete (Trog) Williams and John Amies in 1963.

Best Conditions: It is slippery when wet. The climb can remain damp for some time after a wet spell and is often out of condition throughout most of the winter months.

Approach: *See* introductory notes for Dovedale Church.

Starting Point: Right of the barrier of overhangs, the crag falls back into a huge brown-stained, undercut corner. Start below this.

Descent: By abseil only. The route finishes at a notch in the pinnacles and abseil slings and peg are to the left (south) of this.

This is probably the best VS in Dovedale. Perfect rock and with good protection available. One or two larger nuts may be found useful as the crack is quite wide in places. The crux is probably in the first few moves needed to get established in the corner proper, with another awkward move where it is necessary to move onto the left wall at the bulge.

75: ANACONDA & PHIL'S ROUTE
(HVS, E2) 30m

Summary: Two fine steep lines. Phil's Route crosses an amazing block roof, via a hand-jamming crack, and requires some gymnastic ability to surmount the lip. Protection is excellent, camming devices can get stuck.

First Ascents: Phil's Route – Steve Read, Roy Leeming, Derek Carnell, P. Brown and Steve Hunt in 1956 as an A3 aid route, completely freed by 1970. Anaconda – Roy Leeming in 1965, using 1 point of aid, and freed in the early 1970s by persons unrecorded.

Best Conditions: Being on a pinnacle, the routes can dry fairly quickly but their shady position usually leaves them damp throughout the winter months.

Approach: *See* introductory notes for Dovedale Church.

Starting Points: The river face of Dovedale Church is characterized by a long block overhang. Start Anaconda below a groove at the left end of the overhang. Phil's Route starts below the all too obvious roof crack a little way to the right.

Descent: By abseil only, from a ledge at the back of the pinnacle. Traverse round the downstream end of Dovedale Church and continue down and along between the two groups of pinnacles to pegs and slings close to the finish of Snakes Alive. Abseil into the gap. Other descents are not recommended.

Like something from the lost world, Dovedale Church rises from the forest, a strange tangle of archways and towers, time-worn and timeless.

Anaconda gives a fine introduction to the pinnacles and to finding the abseil. Steep and well protected, with the usual *mélange* of grass and rock to finish. It is possible to finish up cracks as for Phil's Route, at the same grade but with better protection.

Phil's Route can provide endless amusement, particularly if you are in the audience. Crossing the roof is relatively simple, but rounding the lip is not and many an aspirant rock star has been lowered ignominiously into the nettles. It is all too easy to fill the crack with gear and leave no room for the hands. Once round the lip, laybacking pays better dividends than jamming, and knees are definitely allowed. Most climbers just fall off.

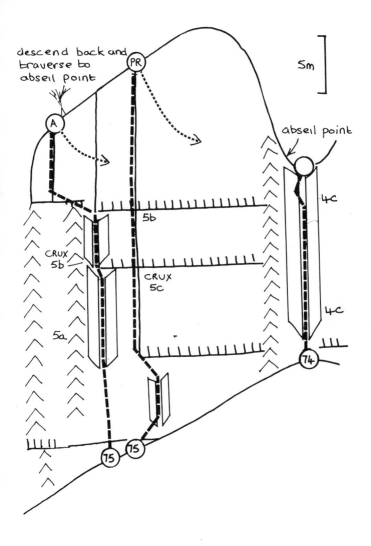

descend back and
traverse to
abseil point

PR

5m

A

abseil point

4c

5b

CRUX
5b

CRUX
5c

5a

4c

74

75   75

Manifold Valley Area

The Manifold Valley is in Staffordshire and runs roughly parallel to, and west of, Dovedale. Despite geographical similarities, the two valleys are quite different in character and, while Dovedale is filled with the endless bustle of trippers up and down the riverside, the Manifold Valley manages to maintain a certain air of tranquillity despite its popularity. The River Manifold rises north of Buxton on Axe Edge but during much of its travels along the Valley it disappears into subterranean passageways, only rising to the stream bed during wet weather. A small road runs along the north end of the Valley and one cuts across the Valley between the villages of Wetton and Grindon but a disused railway track along the valley floor provides access to the crags for pedestrians and cyclists.

Although the Manifold Valley does not hold the concentration of crags found in Dovedale, it contains some excellent climbing, on perfect, pocketed rock. The bowl-shaped crags of Beeston Tor can be a perfect sun-trap even in the short winter days.

Approaches: The Manifold Valley is not readily accessible to those without transport, lying well away from the routes of public transport. From the A515 Buxton to Ashbourne road, take the Milldale road at SK 154549, cross the River Dove and continue to Alstonfield. Leave the village on the south side, follow signs for Wetton, do not turn into the village but continue towards Grindon. The road drops down steep hairpin bends into the Valley at Weag's Bridge with car parking space beyond, on the right.

From the car-park, Beeston Tor is 500m downstream, Thor's Cave 1km upstream. *See* relevant crag Approaches.

Accommodation: Camping – at Alstonfield, Wetton Mill, and in the field below Beeston Tor.
B. & b. – available at many pubs and farms in the area.
Bivouacs – there are no outstanding sites in the Manifold Valley but Thor's Cave would provide some rather draughty shelter, as would Chimney Crag at SK 096556 close to the footpath.

Services: The nearest town is Ashbourne, some 4km along the A515 past the junction for Thorpe. Wetton, Alstonfield and Hartington have post offices. The closest shops are probably in Ashbourne. There is a snack bar at Milldale, a café at Wetton Mill and toilets at Milldale and Wetton Mill car-park. Alstonfield, Grindon and Wetton all have pubs. Petrol is obtainable in Hartington, Thorpe and at Newhaven on the A515. There is a Mountain Rescue Post at Ilam Hall, Ilam.

A Concise History: Recorded climbing in the Manifold Valley seems to have started in 1952 with Joe Brown and Ron Moseley's ascent of The Thorn on Beeston Tor. Around this time the Rock and Ice Club and The Oread paid the valley several visits and successes included aided versions of West Window Groove and Tower Direct. They also aided Central Route and The Curtain on Thor's Cave, the lines of which were later climbed free. On Beeston Tor, The Ivy Gash was climbed by John Sumner, Tony Moulam and Dave Alcock, using aid. It was not until the mid 1960s that the free climbing potential of the valley started to be realized.

in 1965 G. Smith and T. Burnell climbed Beeston Eliminate using 2 points of aid, Nat Allen and D. Burgess free climbed Central Wall and West Wall Climb on Beeston Tor and, by the late 1960s, climbers such as Des Hadlum, G. Smith, Paul Nunn and Trevor Briggs were making regular first ascents with the odd point of aid. A long-standing problem on Beeston Tor was the all too obvious line now taken by The Beest. Patience, which climbs part of the starting groove, had earlier been climbed by Hadlum and Smith but the full challenge was eventually accepted in 1970 by Jeff Morgan and Z. Dyszlewicz (Black Fred). Six points of aid were used on the first ascent and the route was not freed until 1977. On Thor's Cave in 1971, Tom Proctor and Chris Jackson ascended Tower Direct to give a tremendous free climb – a typical Proctor calling card. Development slowed to a trickle for a few years, with the only notable achievement being the ascent of The Black Grub on Beeston Tor by J. Yates and the Dale brothers, Brian and Steve. A superb and bold ascent, a peg was placed by hand in the steep and sustained crux from which the leader climbed down for a rest. On returning, he had the strength to hit it only twice before climbing past it. The peg subsequently fell out.

Later, in the 1970s, Catharsis, a counter route to Black Grub, was added by Dave Jones and R. Cope, who also added the ever popular Pocket Symphony and Evensong up the pockety wall to the left of Central Wall.

The 1980s produced some hard problems; climbers such as Phil Burke and Mark Elwell tackled the steep headwall of Beeston, and others, like Gary Gibson, worked out some fine problems on the right wing of the crag. The decade closed with a remarkable achievement in Thor's Cave – Andy Pollitt's free ascent of the A3 aid route Kyrie Eleison. Originally claimed to be the longest-aided roof in The Peak, it now clocks in at E7 6b.

THOR'S CAVE

The huge entrance of Thor's Cave and the surrounding towers of rock, high on the rim of the valley, are a conspicuous landmark and popular tourist attraction. The cave has two entrances, the main one and the West Window which leads into a steep gully.

From the car-park, follow the path for 1km upstream. Cross the footbridge and climb the steep hillside to Thor's Cave. Walk inside and turn right through the West Window.

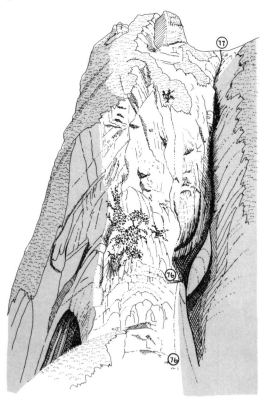

Adey Hubbard on Lime Street Direct (Route 55), Willersley Castle Rocks, Matlock. (Photo: Chris Jackson.)

76: TOWER DIRECT & DEEP FREEZE (E3, E2) 35m

Summary: Tower Direct is a tremendous climb up the thin flake in the centre of the west wall. Deep Freeze is an enjoyable excursion up the wall to the left of Tower Direct and, despite its name, gets the available afternoon sunshine in the summer.

First Ascents: Tower Direct – Roy Leeming, at some time in the 1950s as an A1 aid route, and free climbed by Tom Proctor and Chris Jackson in July 1971. Deep Freeze – Gary Gibson, Mark Elwell and Phil Gibson in October 1983.

Best Conditions: The West Window is a draughty place, and the routes are best climbed in warm, summer conditions when the afternoon sun reaches the depths of the Window.

Approach: *See* introductory notes for Thor's Cave.

Starting Point: Tower Direct – in the top of the gully, below the West Window, it is possible to scramble up to a comfortable belay ledge at 6m. Deep Freeze – can be traversed into from the same belay ledge. However, traditionally it starts below a broken, wide crack reached from further down the gully.

Descent: Walk back until it is possible to descend to the left side (facing in) of the main entrance. It is also possible to descend to West Window gully by traversing to the right to reach a small but well-worn track.

Tower Direct gives some tremendous climbing up the steep south wall of the gully. Once started, there is no real resting place until the top is reached, although thankfully it is possible to arrange some excellent protection between the bits of tatty *in situ* gear. The crux comes about half-way up the left-hand flake where failing strength and steepening rock can combine to produce that inevitable sag onto a runner. The pitch steepens for the final crack but a little perseverance will allow good holds and a welcome hand jam to be gained just below easier ground.

Taking Deep Freeze by either start, the really enjoyable climbing starts at the steep white wall left of the small overhang. Every move looks a little unlikely until you try it, when superb little incuts always come to hand. Keep left of the *in situ* tat on the steep section and this eventually leads to a delectable finishing groove at a more reasonable angle.

As with all the routes on Thor's Cave, belays are hard to find on the summit and it is probably safer to engineer something below the top at the end of the difficulties, this also allows one to maintain verbal contact with the second.

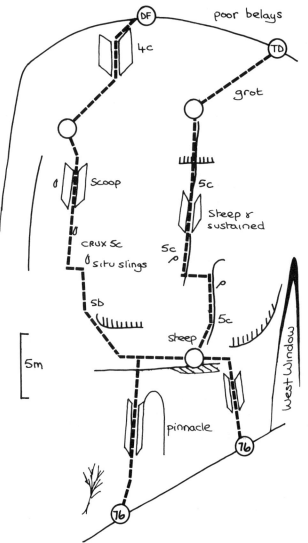

77: WEST WINDOW GROOVE (HVS) 35m

Summary: An excellent exercise in fighting vertigo, up the huge chimney and groove line above the West Window.

First Ascent: Joe Brown and Ron Moseley in the early 1950s as an A1 aid route. The first free ascent is not recorded.

Best Conditions: In summer. The route can retain some dampness after a wet spell.

Approach: *See* introductory notes for Thor's Cave.

Starting Point: At easy grooves and ledges up the left side (facing out) of the West Window.

Descent: Walk back until it is possible to descend to the left side (facing in) of the main entrance. It is also possible to descend to West Window gully by traversing to the right to reach a small but well-worn track.

A real limestone classic and much better and less strenuous than appearances would suggest. There is a certain amount of *in situ* gear on the first pitch, and one or two larger camming devices or Hexes will be found useful in the upper cracks. The crux of the first pitch is the deceptively reasonable step into the main groove. It is important that this short traverse is not taken too low or the moves will be found much harder. Above, there are a couple of difficult moves to get started, best tackled by back and foot, facing right, so that the small hand-ledge on the right wall can become a foot-ledge. The climbing gradually eases to the top. Belays are conspicuous by their absence and many parties descend the hillside and sit in a depression in the grass where communication with the second will be found impossible. With care it may be possible to arrange a secure belay below the top.

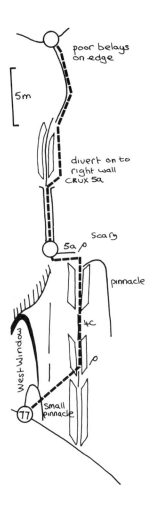

poor belays
on edge

5m

divert on to
right wall
CRUX 5a

Scary

5a ρ

pinnacle

4c

ρ

West Window

77

Small
pinnacle

BEESTON TOR

Beeston Tor ranks as one of the most enjoyable crags in The Peak District. South facing and sheltered, it can be a sun-trap even in the winter months. The crag is broadly concave, characterized by the prominent vertical crack and chimney line of The Thorn and also the curving line of caves at two-thirds height, Ivy Gash. The rock is generally excellent and blessed with numerous sharp solution pockets which often provide excellent holds and which can form natural threads to produce running belays in the most unexpected situations. The lower ramparts of the main face of Beeston Tor tend to be slabby but they progressively steepen and become bulging towards the top. The left end of the buttress retains much of its slabbiness to the top.

Approaches: From the car-park at Weag's Bridge, follow the path down-stream for 500m to Beeston Tor Farm. It is possible to park your car here (for a fee) and to camp (with permission). Cross the stepping stones and continue along the opposite bank of the river to the crag. In the event of high water, paddling may be necessary, although there is a muddy path leading down from the road above Weag's Bridge, through prickly bushes, to the side of the crag.

Roy Small on Black Grub (Route 82), Beeston Tor, Manifold Valley. (Photo: Chris Jackson.)

78: THE BEEST (E3) 71m

Summary: A real limestone classic, two pitches of steep technical climbing in fine position. Protection is excellent throughout. Include some thin tapes or slings for the many natural thread runners on the route, many are *in situ* but may be found in various stages of decay.

First Ascent: Jeff Morgan and Z. Dyszlewicz (Black Fred) in February 1970, using 6 points of aid. Aid was progressively whittled down and the route was completely free by 1977.

Best Conditions: At almost any time. The diagonal crack on pitch 1 may hold a little dampness after a wet spell, as may the main break on pitch 2.

Approach: *See* Approaches under Beeston Tor. Climb the steep bank below the crag to a well-worn patch by a shallow cave, below the huge corner system taken by The Thorn.

Starting Point: A little way to the right of the shallow cave, below an obvious thin groove.

Descent: Walk back from the summit of the crag, then left (facing in) to an easy descent gully.

The first groove is common with Patience (HVS) and so has gained a little extra polish. It is also deceptively steep. However, the hard moves arrive at the bulge where Patience traverses left. There is good protection available but some determination is required to gain the wall above, which despite appearances, provides little in the way of a rest. It is usually with fading arms that the diagonal crack is tackled but a hidden pocket above the break eases the situation and the crack soon leads to easier climbing and the belay.

Above, the climb changes character and steep crack climbing on the first pitch gives way to sweeping white walls. Steep, open climbing is involved on sharp exfoliation flakes and pockets, in tremendous position. There are numerous natural threads for runners, some of which are *in situ* but would stand backing up. The small roof on pitch 2 constitutes the crux of this pitch and requires a long reach to an excellent little jug. Belay in the Holly tree.

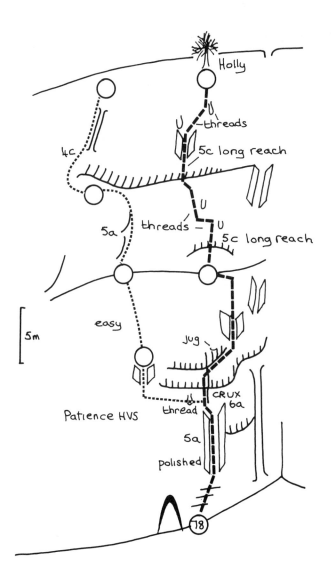

Holly

threads

U

5c long reach

U

threads —   U

5c long reach

jug

easy

5m

CRUX
6a

thread

Patience HVS

5a

polished

18

79: THE THORN (HVS) 49m

Summary: The most travelled route on the crag. From the safe confines of a chimney, pitch 2 traverses out to a steep and exhilarating position.

First Ascent: Joe Brown and Ron Moseley in the early 1950s as an A1 aid route. It was reduced to 2 points of aid by 1965 and completely freed by 1975.

Best Conditions: The easy lower part of the route may retain a little dampness but the crux dries rapidly.

Approach: *See* Approaches under Beeston Tor. Climb the steep bank below the crag to a well-worn patch by a shallow cave.

Starting Point: Right of the prominent crack line at the back of the bay, which leads to the left end of the cave system.

Descent: Walk back across the hillside until it is possible to traverse left (facing in) and down to an easy descent gully.

The most popular route on Beeston Tor and the scene of many minor epics, usually due to lack of communication between leader and second. Pitch 2 traverses from the enclosed safety of the caves of Ivy Gash to a very airy and slightly overhanging rib, giving tremendous views across the buttress. The position is suddenly very exposed but adequately protected by a combination of natural protection and ancient pegs. The crooked line of the pitch means that some care should be taken with rope work to prevent drag. Once on the rib, communication with the second becomes difficult and some sort of pre-arranged signal may be found useful.

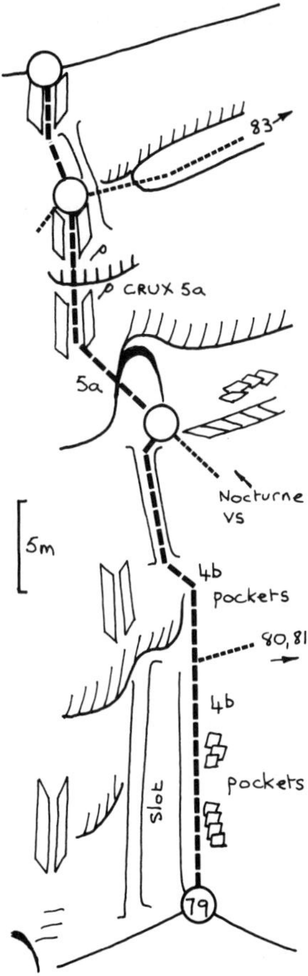

83

CRUX 5a

5a

Nocturne
VS

5m

4b
pockets

80, 81

4b

Slot

pockets

79

80: POCKET SYMPHONY, DEAF DOVE & EVENSONG (E1, E1, E1) 39m, 36m, 38m

Summary: Three delightful exercises in pocket climbing. Much of the protection is by small natural threads, some of these may have *in situ* slings. All routes are fairly low in their grades.

First Ascent: Evensong and Pocket Symphony – Dave Jones and R. Cope in June 1978. Deaf Dove – John Codling in 1979.

Best Conditions: The routes dry fairly rapidly but the pockets can retain small puddles when all else appears to be dry.

Approach: *See* Approaches under Beeston Tor. Climb the steep bank below the crag to a well-worn patch by a shallow cave.

Starting Point: The climbs take the pocketed wall below the caves, right of the first pitch of The Thorn (79) and left of the faint right to left ramp taken by Central Wall (81). Left to right the routes are Pocket Symphony, Deaf Dove and Evensong. Start as for Route 79.

Descent: By abseil. Carefully descend to the sloping floor of the caves of Ivy Gash to an abseil point on The Thorn. If you finished up Ivy Gash, walk back up the hillside until it is possible to traverse left to the descent gully.

Three enjoyable routes that are usually climbed for their second pitches which have many similarities of style. Those with pointed toes may have an advantage in the small pocket holds. Having climbed one route, many parties immediately abseil for the next. The Ivy Gash finish adds another 20m on to the routes and is well worth the trouble, particularly on a first visit to the crag. The cosy recesses of the cave give way to a series of exposed but well-protected moves up a wall and groove, leading back left to a belay bower.

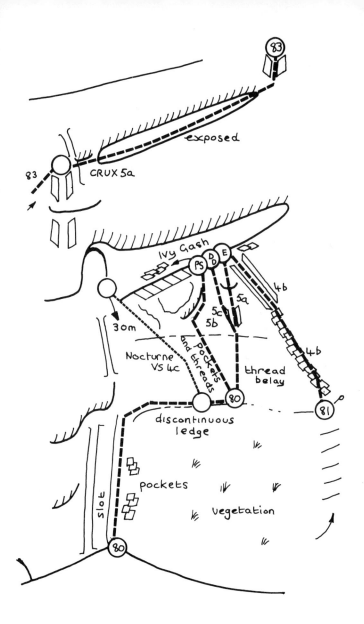

exposed

83

CRUX 5a

Ivy Gash

PS D E
     b

5c   5a
5b

4b

30m

Nocturne
VS 4c

pockets
and threads

thread
belay

4b

80

81

discontinuous
ledge

slot

pockets

vegetation

80

81: CENTRAL WALL (VS) 25m

Summary: The easiest route across the fine slab below the caves of Ivy Gash, sustained and in good position but getting a little polished. For those requiring a little more of a challenge it is possible to finish up Ivy Gash (HVS).

First Ascent: D. Burgess and J. R. (Nat) Allen in 1966.

Best Conditions: It dries fairly quickly, although water streaks may persist across the upper slab.

Approach: *See* Approaches under Beeston Tor. Climb the steep bank below the crag to a well-worn patch by a shallow cave.

Starting Point: From the foot of the steep bank below the shallow cave, take a narrow path leading right, until it is possible to make a scramble up to the right end of the slabs. This can be quite exciting in damp conditions, so take care. Move left to a peg belay. (*See* the topo for Route 82.)

Descent: By abseil. Carefully descend the sloping floor of the caves of Ivy Gash to an abseil point on The Thorn. If you finished up Ivy Gash, walk back up the hillside until it is possible to traverse left to the descent gully.

An enjoyable outing that provides continual interest and takes the easiest-angled line through the steep barrier of slabs below Ivy Gash. Well protected by wires and natural threads, Central Wall is a popular outing and is often combined with the Ivy Gash finish, which is at a slightly higher grade.

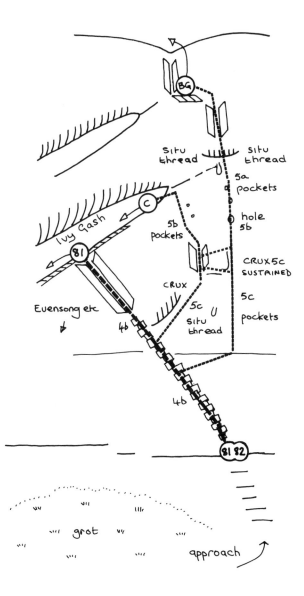

82: BLACK GRUB & CATHARSIS (E3, E3) 25m, 27m

Summary: Black Grub offers steep and exhilarating climbing, following the black streak below the right end of Ivy Gash. Catharsis, which is slightly easier and almost as enjoyable, is also well worth the effort.

First Ascent: Black Grub – J. Yates, B. Dale and S. Dale in 1974 – an impressive first ascent. Legend has it that the peg runner was placed by hand to allow a retreat. On returning for the successful push, the peg was hit twice but was so poor that it fell out as the second approached it. Catharsis – Dave Jones and R. Cope in July 1978.

Best Conditions: This section of wall can retain a wet streak after there has been rain.

Approach: *See* Approaches under Beeston Tor. Climb the steep bank below the crag to a well-worn patch by a shallow cave.

Starting Point: From the foot of the steep bank below the shallow cave (*see* Approach), take a narrow path leading right, until it is possible to make a scramble up to the right end of the slabs to a peg belay, as for Route 81.

Descent: Ascend the grassy hillside behind the belay until it is possible to traverse left into the easy descent gully.

Black Grub must be the best pitch on Beeston Tor and sits towards the top of its grade. Sustained and strenuous, it is a tremendous outing. The steep wall consists of small pockets and only succumbs to a determined approach. Above this, the site of the ill-fated peg now takes an excellent but awkward-to-place wire, and there is no resting place until the uncomfortable niche on the left is reached, also used by Catharsis. This was the original line of the route, which moves back right from the niche, but the route is sometimes climbed direct to the final line of huge pockets and threads which may push the route up to the bottom end of E4. Protection is somewhat spaced on the lower wall, although it is possible to arrange a dubious wire in a pocket and there is a thin thread usually *in situ*. Savour this one – it holds all that is wonderful in limestone climbing. Take it on a crisp autumn day when there is the smell of leaves and a gentle sun in a pale blue English sky.

83: BEESTON ELIMINATE (HVS) 80m

Summary: A fine traverse from left to right across the upper walls of the buttress, a classic from the 1960s. Protection is generally good.

First Ascent: G. Smith and T. Burnell in 1965 using 2 points of aid. The start, which takes pitches 1 and 2 of West Wall Climb, was first climbed by D. Burgess and J. R. (Nat) Allen in 1963.

Best Conditions: The breaks above the traverse line and the start of the last pitch may weep a little after a wet spell.

Approach: *See* Approaches under Beeston Tor.

Starting Point: The route starts at the left toe of the buttress, below a large tree that is above a well-cleaned strip of rock. Scramble up to the tree to start.

Descent: Gain the summit then bear left and down into the easy descent gully. It is possible to make an exposed abseil from the finishing bower.

Once the most popular excursion on Beeston Tor and still very worthy of attention, Beeston Eliminate gives a good introduction to the climbing on Beeston Tor as well as a good view of many of the other routes. Pitches 1 and 2 are a little pedestrian but by pitch 3 all is forgiven. Delectable traversing across the superb white wall on flakes and sharp incuts lead all too soon to the steep little groove and a belay in the thorny rake above. The start to the last pitch originally required 2 points of aid and probably still constitutes the crux of the route, although the moves are well protected. The route continues to involve traversing, in exposed position above the huge roofs which cap the caves of Ivy Gash and give a very airy, though technically straightforward, finish.

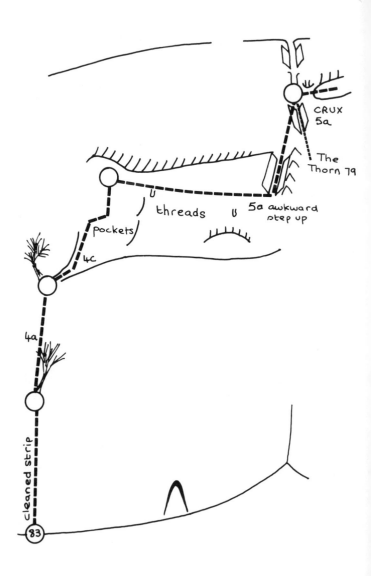

CRUX
5a

The
Thorn 79

threads

pockets

5a awkward
step up

4c

4a

cleaned strip

83

Malham Cove Area

A symbol of the Yorkshire Dales, the great rocky amphitheatre of Malham Cove, is a natural wonder beloved of tourist and climber alike. Once famous for the exploits of the aid man and once deserted save for the rattle of etriers and the sound of the hammer, the bolted, overhanging back wall of the Cove has become tremendously popular amongst aspirant rock stars and is the home of some desperate problems. However, The Right Wing and The Terrace contain many classics of a less demanding nature, which are no less worthy of attention. With a few exceptions, the routes are single pitch, on generally good, sometimes excellent, rock and, owing to the position of the climbs, exposure is often out of all proportion to the length of the route. Because of the shape of the Cove, it can be very sheltered from the wind and a sun-trap in the summer months.

Approaches: Malham Cove lies 1.5km from Malham village and is the source of the River Aire, which re-emerges at its foot as Malham Beck. From Skipton, the nearest small town, follow the A65 west to Gargrave, then turn right along a well-signposted minor road to Malham village. For the western approaches; from Settle follow the A65 east to Gargrave and turn left. For a more scenic route from Settle, there is a minor road which passes Attermire Scars, over the moors, eventually dropping down to Kirby Malham and thence Malham. Both Skipton and Settle can be reached by train, and bus services connect them with Malham.

From Malham village, follow Cove Road in the upstream direction. The Cove is on the right, the approach to which is marked by a well-worn footpath. Parking can be a problem as the Cove is very popular with tourists so be prepared to park in Malham village and walk.

Accommodation: Camping – at Malham and at nearby Gordale.
Youth hostels – at Malham, Stainforth, north of Settle, and at Linton, near Grassington.
B. & b. – available at pubs, farmhouses and cottages in the area.
Bivouacs – it is possible to obtain a sheltered bivouac at the back of the cove beneath the overhanging wall, although this can become unpleasant in wet and windy weather. Beware of falling icicles in the winter months.

Services: There are several cafés, an information centre, a post office, a public telephone and a petrol station in Malham. There are shops in Malham but supplies are best bought in Skipton or Settle.

A Concise History: During the 1950s and early 1960s, Malham Cove was famous for its long and precarious aid routes up the huge back wall of The Cove. In 1959, Pete Biven and Trevor Peck climbed Central Wall in a five-day bolting epic, using modified curtain hooks as hangers. Several aid routes were pioneered around this time but there was also activity on the much more amenable 'wings'. Allan Austin, who was to feature large in the next decade, discovered Terrace Wall, and Brian Evans The Kylin. They then teamed up to climb Pikedaw Wall, Kirkby Wall, East Wall Route and many other now popular routes.

Following the publication of Mike Mitchell's *Climbs on Yorkshire Limestone* (*The Dalesman*, 1963), attention was drawn to Malham Cove and a new generation of climbs began to appear. In 1964, Austin climbed Sarcophagus using 2 points of aid, and Robin Barley and Dennis Gray climbed Wombat, the first true extreme in The Cove, followed by The Macabre, an incredibly bold lead for its day. John Sumner and Dave Sales climbed the Main Overhang and the Right Wing Girdle using some aid. In the mid 1960s, Robin Barleys ascended Carnage. A point of aid was used to start the second pitch and still is by most parties.

The Barley brothers continued to play a dominant role, climbing The Cavern, Crossbones and Carnage Left Hand, and almost freeing the Right Wing Girdle. The 1970s saw the start of climbing on the ludicrously exposed Terrace Wall, with Austin's Sundance Wall, but the way was now open for the next generation of climbers, dominated by Ron Fawcett and Pete Livesey. Fawcett freed Mulatto Wall while Livesey climbed Doubting Thomas on the impressive wall left of Wombat and Pumpwater Meets The Hulk, an exposed traverse across the headwall of Carnage. John Syrett bagged Midnight Cowboy but only just, as the onset of darkness forced the use of an aid point beyond the crux. The obvious ramp left of Doubting Thomas was climbed by Fawcett with a pre-placed peg runner after a ground fall from near the top by Tim Jepson, to give Slender Loris.

During the 1980s, the gaps continued to be filled as harder and more gymnastic routes were pioneered, prominent during this period was the bouldering expert Rob Gawsthorpe. Neil Foster discovered Wild West Hero, Swift Attack and New Dawn Fades at the disappearing end of The Terrace, but perhaps the most radical moves were the interest shown in the bolt ladders on Central Wall. Fawcett was in at the start with the tremendous Yosemite Wall (E5 6a), soon overshadowed by his New Dawn (E6 6c). Development in this area still continues apace.

THE TERRACE

The Terrace is the upper, leftwards extension of the Right Wing gained from the top of the Cove. It is best reached by traversing right, below the Right Wing, until it is possible to scramble up and traverse back left to the top of the Cove.

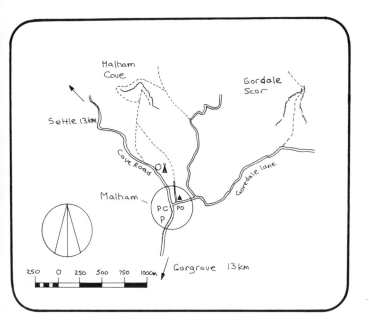

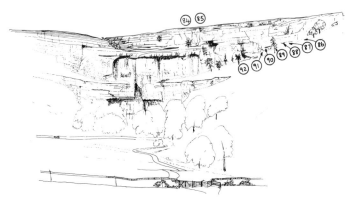

84: SUNDANCE WALL & SWIFT ATTACK (E2, E2) 18m

Summary: The two classics of The Terrace, exposed out of all proportion to their stature. Steep and 'pumpy' in the lower reaches but easier going as height is gained. Protection is good on both routes, if you can hang on long enough to arrange it.

First Ascents: Sundance Wall – Allan Austin and Frank Wilkinson in 1970. So exposed is this route that Austin wore a prusik loop on the rope during the first ascent for fear of ending up over the big drop. Swift Attack – Neil Foster in 1983.

Best Conditions: At almost any time, but as with all the routes on The Terrace it can be draughty when the wind blows from the south.

Approach: *See* Approaches under Malham Cove. From the top of The Cove, scramble down to a spacious area overlooking the big drop, where a diminishing grassy ledge leads off to the left (facing out).

Starting Point: Follow the grassy ledge down an exposed step to a broadening at a cave with a huge thread. Sundance starts at the right end of the cave, 3m right of the thread; Swift Attack starts some 3m further right where a hanging belay can be arranged.

Descent: Walk back and left to join the normal approach and scramble down into the dry valley above the Cove.

With both routes, the first 5–6m constitutes the crux of the climb but it is possible to arrange some good protection, an essential requirement for most parties as the lower bulging section of the route overhangs the belay ledge. Good wire placements can usually be found in the bulge left of a shallow groove and about 5m above the ledge. The two routes are close here and many climbers end up on common ground, but with no loss of quality. Above, on Sundance, an enormous thread/jug makes for a very welcome breather. Swift Attack moves right from here and, although the angle soon eases, there are still one or two entertaining moves remaining before the top is reached.

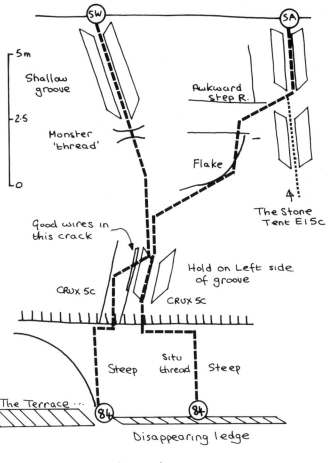

SW

SA

5m

Shallow
groove

Awkward
step R.

2·5

Monster
'thread'

Flake

The Stone
Tent E15c

0

Good wires in
this crack

Hold on Left side
of groove

CRUX 5c

CRUX 5c

Steep

Situ
thread

Steep

The Terrace ···

84

84

Disappearing ledge

Big Drop ↓

85: MIDNIGHT COWBOY (E3) 20m

Summary: A wonderful outing on perfect rock with some intimidating climbing in the middle section of the route. A couple of small-to-medium (1–1½) sized camming devices may be found useful in the upper flake crack.

First Ascent: John Syrett in 1972, with 1 point of aid above the crux due to the onset of darkness.

Best Conditions: At almost any time, although the route can be exposed to the wind.

Approach: *See* Approaches to Malham Cove and introductory notes to Terrace Wall.

Starting Point: From the cave with the giant thread, hand traverse right to a tree, then continue more easily to a slight widening below a flake, some 6m right of the tree. Most parties use a rope across this section.

Descent: Walk back and left to join the normal approach and scramble down into the dry valley above The Cove.

An exciting little number in a stunning position. The central part of the route is generally considered to constitute the crux, if only psychologically, and consists of a rising traverse up a steep grey ramp. Protection is conspicuous by its absence across this section although there are good wire placements at either end of the ramp, and a semi-resting place below the flakes. The flakes, although technically easier than the rest of the route, are strenuous and should not be underestimated.

THE RIGHT WING

The Right Wing is the rightwards extension of Malham Cove and contains some of its most accessible and popular routes.

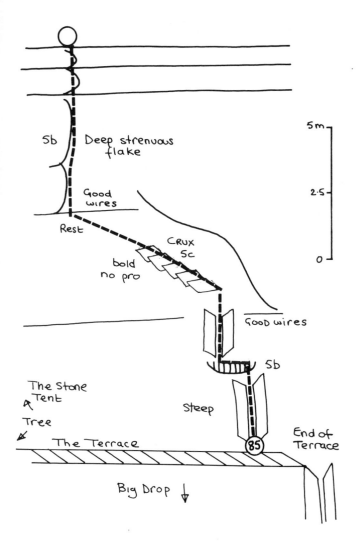

5m

2.5

0

5b   Deep strenuous flake

Good wires

Rest

CRUX 5c

bold no pro

Good wires

5b

The Stone Tent

Tree

The Terrace

Steep

85

End of Terrace

Big Drop ↓

86: PIKEDAW WALL (VS) 20m

Summary: Traditionally graded VS, this steep little route should be regarded as being towards the top of its grade. It can be well protected.

First Ascent: Brian Evans and Allan Austin in 1961.

Best Conditions: It dries quickly at most times of the year.

Approach: *See* Approaches under Malham Cove. Approach to the Right Wing routes is by following the tourist route from Malham village until below the huge back wall of the Cove. From here a path zig-zags up the hillside to the right end of the crag where there is a useful, detached boulder which serves as a popular gearing up point.

Starting Point: A prominent feature of this part of the Right Wing is the steep leaning corner of The Cavern, leading to two small caves on the upper wall. Right of the corner are two grooves, the smaller left one being capped by a roof. Start below the right-hand one.

Descent: Walk to the right (facing in) along the top of the Cove and descend at the end where a very polished stone wall abuts the crag.

A fine little route but not to be underestimated. The moves into and out of the groove are steep and quite strenuous and the polish on the holds necessitates some precise footwork. Except for those with enormous reach, leaving the groove probably constitutes the crux and for most climbers the jug requires a determined pull from a fully extended position.

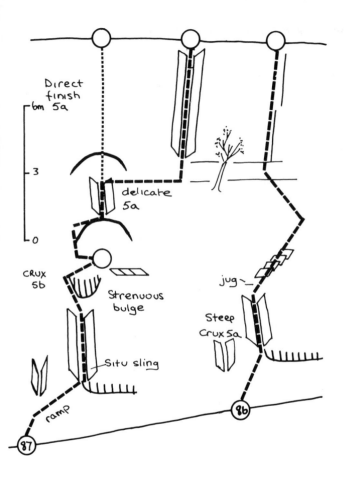

Direct finish
6m 5a

delicate
5a

CRUX
5b

Strenuous
bulge

jug ~

Steep
Crux 5a

Situ sling

ramp

87

86

87: THE CAVERN (HVS) 24m

Summary: A useful introduction to the climbing at Malham Cove, combining sections of delicate footwork with strenuous overhangs on both pitches.

First Ascent: Tony and Robin Barley in the mid 1960s, using 1 point of aid on pitch 1, and later freed by Allan Austin.

Best Conditions: It rarely stays wet for long but is best avoided if damp streaks are present across the slab on pitch 1.

Approach: As for Route 86.

Starting Point: To the right of the detached boulder at the left end of a slab, leading to a prominent overhanging corner below a small cave.

Descent: Walk to the right (facing in) along the top of the Cove and descend at the end where a very polished stone wall abuts the crag.

An interesting mixture of bold slabs and thuggish but well protected overhangs. Most leaders will probably find the slabs to be the most demanding constituents of the route, seconds will probably see things differently. The vintage peg and tat in the well-cracked overhanging corner looks like a Barley original and is unlikely to stand much more than the weight of a karabiner.

88: KIRKBY WALL (HVS) 30m

Summary: A justifiably popular route but now becoming rather polished in its lower section which it shares with The Kylin (HVS 5b, 4c). The upper wall contains some excellent climbing on perfect rock.

First Ascent: Brian Evans and Allan Austin in 1961.

Best Conditions: It dries fairly quickly but the overhangs on pitch 1 can weep after prolonged rain making the route much harder.

Approach: As for Route 86.

Starting Point: Start above the detached boulder, at the left side of a shallow cave below a series of thin grooves leading to a line of roofs.

Descent: Walk to the right (facing in) along the top of the Cove and descend at the end where a very polished stone wall abuts the crag.

One of the best excursions at its grade on The Right Wing, just slightly marred by the mirror-like polish on the first few holds. Reaching the traverse line is regarded as the crux by some parties and, indeed, could be desperate in the damp, although some *in situ* protection can often be found here. However, the best part of the route is to follow: a delectable traverse leads to a well-positioned stance below the final wall. The line of the route, though a little devious, contains some fine climbing and a couple of deceptively awkward moves where the route steps right from the corner.

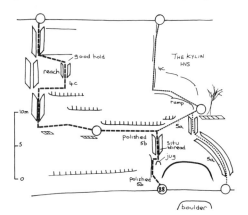

89: WOMBAT (E2) 27m

Summary: Steep and exciting climbing with a difficult entry and a strenuous and exposed crux situated just below the top.

First Ascent: Robin Barley and Dennis Gray in 1964, probably the first Extreme climbed in Malham Cove.

Best Conditions: At almost any time as it dries fairly quickly.

Approach: As for Route 86.

Starting Point: Above the detached boulder is the shallow cave marking the start of Kirkby Wall. Left from here is an undercut section of rock which ends at a wall leading to a left-facing groove.

Descent: Walk to the right (facing in) along the top of the Cove and descend at the end where a very polished stone wall abuts the crag.

This beast pulls no punches right from the start and probably represents the top of its grade. The entry into the groove requires some determination and clean boots to combat the polish. Fortunately, the moves are protectable by a good wire in the overhang. The climbing gradually steepens until just below the final wall, in sight of the summit fence-post. The moves are strenuous and committing, and involve first reaching a finger flake out left, which will take a small wire and then the break above which will take a camming device. From there on it is up or off. Originally there was a thin flake just below the top which provided sharp finger holds, all that remains now is a faint scar. Two small pockets provide just adequate purchase and, with fading fingers, allow that final reach out left into a good jug and thence the top.

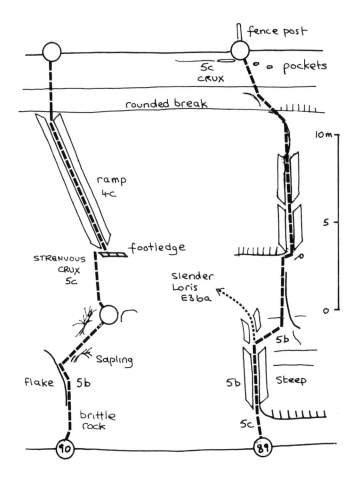

fence post

5c
CRUX

pockets

rounded break

10m

ramp
4c

5

footledge

STRENUOUS
CRUX
5c

Slender
Loris
E3 ba

0

Sapling

5b

Flake   5b

5b   Steep

brittle
rock

5c

90   89

90: CROSSBONES (E2) 29m

Summary: Excellent climbing, steep and strenuous and in tremendous position; epitomizing all that is best in Yorkshire limestone.

First Ascent: Tony and Robin Barley in the mid 1960s.

Best Conditions: It is not particularly prone to seepage and tends to dry quickly after a wet spell.

Approach: As for Route 86.

Starting Point: Left of the detached boulder, the crag continues to a prominent cut-away corner, the start to Carnage Left Hand. Start a few metres right of the corner, below a flake leading to a sapling.

Descent: Walk to the right (facing in) along the top of the Cove and descend at the end where a very polished stone wall abuts the crag.

The upper pitch of Crossbones must rate amongst the most satisfying on the right wing of Malham Cove. The crux consists of a series of increasingly fingery moves to reach a rather rounded break. Good protection can be arranged at the crux using several small wires, although one of them fits behind what seems to be a piece of detached limestone. Once established round the overhanging section, the upper wall is pure delight, following an exquisite ramp, straightforward after the crux section but well worth savouring. Smallish wires (2, 3, 4) will be found useful on the upper wall, so one or two extras, beyond a standard rack, may be required for this pitch.

91: CARNAGE LEFT HAND (E1) 60m

Summary: Probably one of the two most famous routes in Malham Cove, a reputation well deserved for the climbing on the fine upper wall. Carnage and Carnage Left Hand share some common ground at the section above the roof of the cave but are essentially independent routes.

First Ascent: Tony and Robin Barley in the mid 1960s. One point of aid was used to surmount the guardian overhang at the start of pitch 3 and still is by most parties. It was freed by Ron Fawcett in the early 1970s at 6b.

Best Conditions: The upper wall dries quickly after rain but the starting corner may retain some dampness.

Approach: As For Route 86.

Starting Point: Left of the detached boulder, the crag continues to a prominent cut-away corner leading to grass ledges and bushes.

Descent: Walk to the right (facing in) along the top of the Cove and descend at the end where a very polished stone wall abuts the crag.

A delightful expedition, progressively increasing in difficulty and culminating in the fine headwall which is found by most parties to be slightly easier than the line taken by Carnage.

The start is shared with Scorpio, a pleasant HVS which meanders its way up the corner above and right of the belay tree. Pitch 2 of Carnage Left Hand traverses out left from the belay and soon gives a first taste of the exposure to be experienced on the final pitch. The traverse, though graded 5b, is not high in its grade and can be adequately protected by smallish wires. The *pièce de résistance* is, of course, the headwall and the first problem is getting established around the guardian roof. For those not at ease with 6b, a fairly short sling will be needed on the peg just round the lip, in order to reach good holds. Once established and suitably blinkered from the exposure the climbing is pure delight, first following Carnage and then traversing left into a series of short corners which lead all too soon to the top.

92: MULATTO WALL (E3) 48m

Summary: Two excellent pitches of contrasting character. Protection can be a little spaced on the first pitch but the crux is protected by a peg and an ancient bolt.

First Ascent: First climbed free by Ron Fawcett in the mid 1970s.

Best Conditions: Both pitches dry fairly quickly after rain.

Approach: As for Route 86.

Starting Point: Left of the boulder, the upper tier of the Cove extends downwards to a disappearing terrace. A little way along this is a small grassy upper ledge with an ash tree at its left end. Start behind this.

Descent: Walk to the right (facing in) along the top of the Cove and descend at the end where a very polished stone wall abuts the crag.

Indifferent rock at the start of pitch 1 soon gives way to some absorbing climbing round the two pieces of *in situ* gear, an ancient peg and a bolt of similar vintage. The crux consists of pocket pulls between the *in situ* gear, though the unprotected but easier traverse out left may be considered by some to be more of a problem. The climbing soon eases to about 5a and a belay is usually taken well left at the tree in the caves used by Carnage. The rope work from this belay to the start of pitch 2 can cause some problems and it is important to ensure that protection inserted in the lower part of the upper pitch will withstand a sideways pull without dislodging. It is also difficult to avoid a lot of slack in the system without dragging your partner off the rock. It may be possible to engineer a sound but hanging belay in the upper part of pitch 1 thus avoiding problems with rope management.

These problems apart, pitch 2 of Mulatto is a superb experience, steep but protectable and on perfect limestone. The pitch traverses left to share the 'mantelshelf' of Carnage and finishes as for that route.

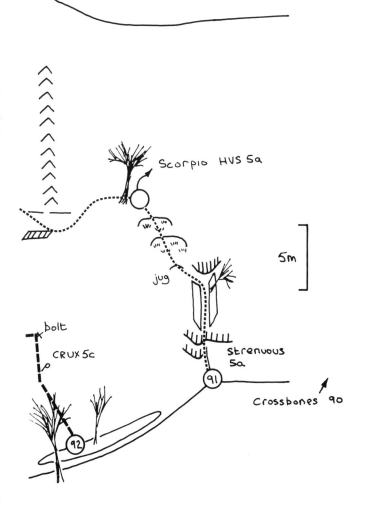

Scorpio HVS 5a

jug

5m

bolt

CRUX 5c

Strenuous
5a

91

Crossbones 90

92

93: CARNAGE (E2) 46m

Summary: A 'must' for any competent visiting party. The slightly grim lower pitch contrasts delightfully with the joyous upper wall.

First Ascent: Carnage – Tony and Robin Barley in the mid 1960s. As with Carnage Left Hand, 1 point of aid was used to surmount the guardian overhang at the start of pitch 2, and still is by most parties. It was freed by Ron Fawcett in the early 1970s at 6b.

Best Conditions: The upper wall dries quickly but the lower wall may retain a little dampness in the upper crack after a spell of rain.

Approach: As for Route 86.

Starting Point: Left of the starting corner of Carnage Left Hand, the crag extends downwards. Start above a prominent oak tree and below an obvious ledge at 4m: above is a black bulge topped by tree-filled caves.

Descent: Walk to the right (facing in) along the top of the Cove and descend at the end where a very polished stone wall abuts the crag.

The first moves make the start of pitch 1 an uneasy experience on a first visit, as protection is conspicuous by its absence and though the first ledge contains some good holds they are not exactly above suspicion. Once established on the ledge, normality returns and the remainder of the pitch is far less intimidating than appearances might suggest. An ancient ring peg at the end of the traverse allows a welcome back rope for the second man on The Macabre, a scary E3 5b, which traverses out left from here.

The top pitch of Carnage provides climbing in a tremendous position, steep and protectable on perfect rock – once you have overcome the initial overhang that is. Most parties choose to stand in a short sling from the peg just round the roof, thus enabling good holds to be reached out left, otherwise it's apparently 6b. The top pitch of Carnage is also famous for its mantelshelf move, immortalized in Ken Wilson's book *Hard Rock* (Hart-Davis, MacGibbon Ltd., 1975). Only those wishing to upgrade the move to 6a will choose this technique as a good finger hold high up on the left allows the ledge to be stepped onto at around 5b.

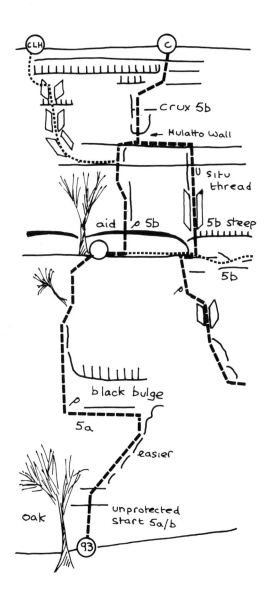

GORDALE SCAR

This deep and impressive scar is really a gorge and was probably once part of a cave system. Inside, the river cascades down two steep steps, the lower of which is usually negotiable except in times of flood. The inner reaches of Gordale are dark and overhanging and prone to seepage and, with one notable exception, Light, contain some very hard routes. The outer reaches of Gordale are wider, less steep and catch available afternoon sun, and although the rock quality is variable in places, the crag is an essential visit for any competent party.

Gordale is a major tourist attraction with hundreds of people walking through it on busy days. Some of the routes, including Light, lie close to the path and it is **very important** to avoid any risk to the public, the most likely danger being falling rocks. Utmost caution is urged, an accident could cost a life and lose future access to the crag. Occasionally there may be access restrictions to the crags due to the nesting of rare birds. Details of the situation are available in the Old Barn Café, Malham.

Approaches: Approach as for Malham Cove but in the village turn right over a small bridge, pass The Lister's Arms and Malham Café and follow the small road, keeping right at the junction. The road first climbs then drops down to a small bridge over Gordale Beck. Parking is usually possible here. The crag can be found by following the path up by the beck for 1km.

Accommodation and Services: As for Malham Cove.

94: FACE ROUTE (E3) 47m

Summary: A superb climb. By far
the best route of its grade in Gordale and a taste of the harder stuff
that the Gorge offers. Well protected, with many old pegs *in situ*.

First Ascent: Ron Moseley and J.
Mortimer as an aid route in 1956,
and climbed free by Pete Livesey
and John Sheard in October 1971.

Best Conditions: The route catches the afternoon sun for most of
the year and this can be worth waiting for as Gordale can be a
draughty place. The lower 12m are
sometimes wet due to seepage
from the first roof, although the
climbing is less demanding on this
section.

Approach: *See* Approaches under
Gordale Area. Follow the stream to
where the Gorge narrows.

Starting Point: From where the
left wall of the Gorge (true right
wall) drops straight into the stream,
scramble up and left to the foot of
a flaky corner leading to an obvious
small roof.

Descent: The usual descent is by
a free abseil from the sturdy yew
tree just below the true finish of the
route. The alternative is a long traverse left past the Left Wing Crags
until it is possible to scramble
down.

Essential Gordale for any competent visiting party. The numerous bits of
rusting tat tell of its history as an aid route but now as a free climb it is a
far finer route, although the rusting pegs make for comforting runners. The
crux of the route is on pitch 2 and the problem consists of climbing out
of a shallow cave. The holds above seem close but without a strenuous
undercling and lock off they are frustratingly out of reach. Those with a long
reach may well have an advantage; for those of more modest proportions it
may be comforting to know that protection is at head height.

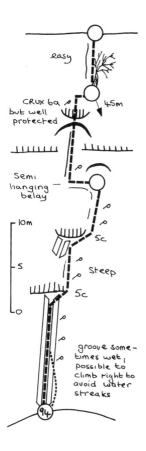

easy

CRUX 6a
but well
protected

45m

Semi
hanging
belay

10m

5c

5

steep

0

5c

groove some-
times wet,
possible to
climb right to
avoid water
streaks

94

95: LIGHT (E1) 35m

Summary: A steep and atmospheric route with a problematic start which can be well protected. Positions in the upper part of the route become quite exciting.

First Ascent: Eric Wallis and Des Hadlum in 1964. This was years ahead of its time and the first major free route in Gordale.

Best Conditions: The start of the route can retain some dampness even after a dry spell. This makes the initial moves somewhat desperate. The upper reaches dry more rapidly but as the route is generally in shadow it can retain dampness for some time.

Approach: *See* Approaches under Gordale Area. Ascend the lower falls and follow the stream for a few metres, past a hanging arête on the right.

Starting Point: Start at a niche below thin, steep cracks on the left side of the arête.

Descent: Either climb the grassy hillside until it is possible to traverse well to the left to easier ground, or make a free abseil from the small tree at the top of the route. Take great care not to dislodge any stones.

Despite its gloomy situation, Light gives a splendid outing with a problematic start guarding the fine upper features. The name Light at first seems to be contradictory until one sees the neighbouring route, Darkness, which takes the evil black cave/chimney system to its left. In dry conditions the start requires some determination and in the damp the odd invocation or metal handhold might be required. Protection is excellent and just when all appears lost there is a perfect finger lock in the crack. Above, things soon ease. The upper pitch is quite a different beast and somewhat easier climbing follows huge features to an exhilarating traverse below a large roof. Protection can always be arranged and some larger nuts or camming devices may be found useful higher up on pitch 2. Some long extenders and a little care with rope technique will prevent drag.

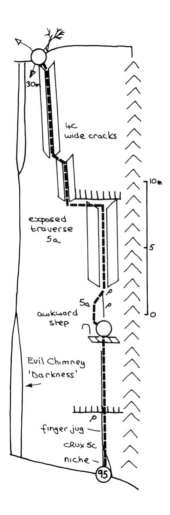

30m

4c wide cracks

10m

exposed
traverse
5a

5

5a

awkward
step

0

Evil Chimney
'Darkness'

finger jug
crux 5c
niche

95

The Western Crags Area

One of the crags that lies in the west of the Yorkshire Dales is Crummack-dale. It is near the village of Austwick, between Settle and Clapham, marked as White Stone on the 1:25,000 OS map. It is a pleasant and peaceful place, faces west and offers extensive views out towards the Solway Firth. Crummackdale Crag is an escarpment on the edge of a moor of bare rocks and limestone pavements and sports some slab routes, which are rarities on limestone crags.

Approaches: The village of Austwick lies 7km north of Settle, off the main A65 trunk road. The 580 Skipton to Lancaster bus stops at Austwick village. From Austwick, follow the Horton road north-east for 2km to a point near a barn and a small stream where there is limited parking. Take the second private road on the left and follow this through the small village of Wharfe, past two barns to an iron gate on the right. Enter the field here and follow the wall leftwards into a larger field then walk up screes to the crag.

Access: The crag is on private land without public right of access and, out of courtesy, the owner is anxious that permission should be sought before climbing there. Access is not usually refused. Contact Mr Morphet, Town End (south-west), Austwick, tel: Clapham 2880.

Accommodation: Camping – at Settle and near Clapham Station (2km south-west of Clapham, across the main A65).
Youth hostels – at Stainforth and Ingleton.
B. & b. – available at pubs and private houses.

Services: Settle is the largest village in the area and most commodities can be obtained. Pubs abound, there are several cafés in both Ingleton and Settle and a Little Chef on the main A65, near the Austwick junction.

A Concise History: Crummackdale first attracted attention in 1959 when Brian Evans climbed Venus and many other of the easier routes. In 1964, Allan Austin and Ernie Goodyear visited the crag on a number of occasions and added many more routes including the delightful Olympus. New routes continued to trickle in over the next six or seven years. Notable in this period are P. Hays and D. Cunningham's ascent of the traverse Jaywalk. In 1971, the Firth brothers opened up the crag towards the right-hand end with their fine route, aptly named Brothers, but they used an aid move. It was not until 1984 that this was eliminated by Steve Rhodes and Steve Aisthorpe, who also both climbed Little Pink Clare and later, with Bruce Jardine, added Feeling The Pinch.

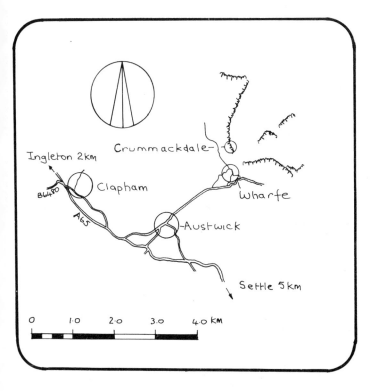

96: OLYMPUS, VENUS & LITTLE PINK CLARE (VS, VS, VS) 32m, 32m, 21m

Summary: Three exquisite slab routes on near perfect rock. Protection is just adequate, despite the roughness and serrations. Runners are not always immediately to hand. A few very small wires may be found useful.

First Ascents: Venus – Brian Evans in 1959. Olympus – Allan Austin and Ernie Goodyear in 1964. Little Pink Clare – Steve Rhodes and Steve Aisthorpe in 1984.

Best Conditions: The crag faces west and is in an exposed position so it can receive a fair amount of weather and strong winds. It is at its best on calm, sunny winter afternoons or at almost any time during fair weather in the summer months. The crag dries quickly after rain.

Approach: *See* Approaches under The Western Crags Area

Starting Points: Olympus and Venus – about 50m left of the stone wall at an obvious rightwards-pointing flake below a slab. Little Pink Clare – below a triangular overhang 10m to the right.

Descent: Walk to the right (facing in) along the top of the crag. It is possible to scramble down the crag some 60m beyond the wall but it is safer to walk inland to a sheepfold where a stile will be found, giving access to the end of the crag.

Originally graded HVS, these routes provide enjoyable climbing and should be on everyone's hit list. Although the routes are each given VS in this guide, Venus may be found fairly high in its grade due to a series of poorly protected moves along the rising traverse, and clean sticky boots will pay dividends here. It is possible to arrange protection for these moves by borrowing a bit of Olympus and descending to the traverse line. Boldness is soon rewarded by better holds and runners.

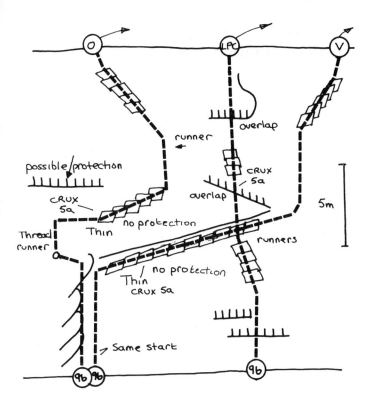

97: BROTHERS & FEELING THE PINCH (E1, E1) 27m, 19m

Summary: In contrast to the previous routes, two routes with testing little overhangs to finish.

First Ascents: Brothers – the Firth brothers in 1971, using 1 aid point, and freed by Steve Rhodes and Steve Aisthorpe in 1984, who climbed Feeling The Pinch at around the same time.

Best Conditions: The crag faces west and is in an exposed position, so it can receive a fair amount of weather and strong winds. It is best on calm, sunny winter afternoons or at almost any time during fair weather in the summer months. The crag dries quickly after rain.

Approach: *See* Approaches under The Western Crags Area

Starting Point: Brothers – 8m left of the stone wall at some flakes. Feeling The Pinch – 5m right of the stone wall below a pinch grip at 4m.

Descent: Walk to the right (facing in) along the top of the crag. It is possible to scramble down the crag some 60m beyond the wall but it is safer to walk inland to a sheepfold where a stile will be found, giving access to the end of the crag.

These are fun routes with thought-provoking finishes. The start of Feeling The Pinch would probably constitute the crux were it at the top of the route. The overhangs, though strenuous, can be adequately protected and the difficulties are soon over.

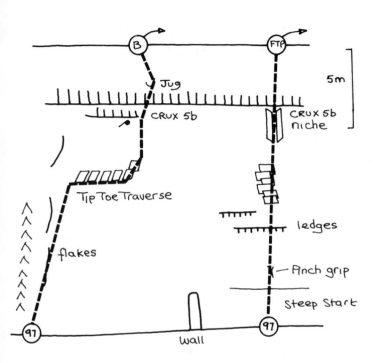

B

FTP

5m

Jug

CRUX 5b

CRUX 5b
niche

Tip Toe Traverse

ledges

flakes

Pinch grip

Steep Start

97

Wall

97

The Eastern Crags

The eastern crags of the Yorkshire Dales contain some of the most serious and difficult routes in the country, but among these are a small number of middle-grade gems. Two crags are included here, Kilnsey Crag and Loup Scar, with the hope that the two areas can be combined to give a memorable day's climbing. The crags are within easy connection for those with transport, Kilnsey being some 7km north of Grassington, and Loup Scar 3km south. For those without transport, I admit that the connection might be a problem.

KILNSEY CRAG

Kilnsey crag is the jutting wall of limestone which seems to overhang the main road between Skipton and Kettlewell in upper Wharfedale. The crag reaches 60m in height and, once dominated by the aid climber, now contains some of the hardest and most spectacular free climbs in the country. Most of the routes are beyond the scope of this guide but there remain one or two in the middle grades which are worthy of inclusion by any visiting party.

At the time of writing there were some access problems, so **please** do not block the road by parking directly below the crag, do not take your dog to the crag or you will be thrown off by the farmer, and do not obstruct the access to his fields. If approached by the farmer, please be polite. There is car parking and sometimes a tea wagon in the lay-by 200m beyond the north end of the crag.

Approaches: The crag is adjacent to the small village of Kilnsey on the B6160, some 20km north of Skipton. From Skipton or the Skipton by-pass, follow signs to Grassington or Kettlewell. The crag is difficult to miss, as it lives up to its nickname, the 'Big Umbrella'.

Accommodation: Camping – on the road to Arncliff at GR SD949704 and off Skirethorns Lane at GR SD972641, near Grassington. A few hundred metres north of Kilnsey Crag there is a camping Barn. Ask for permission at North Cote Farm.
Youth hostels – at Linton, south-west of Grassington, and at Kettlewell.
B. & b. – available at many of the farms and pubs in the area.

Services: The nearest large village is Grassington, where shops, petrol, pubs, cafés and a post office can be found. Skipton is the nearest small town, which offers most commodities and has a railway station.

A Concise History: The history of Kilnsey crag, like many of the steeper limestone outcrops, is a story of aid routes and the progressive movement to raise them to free status. Climbing, or attempts at climbing, on Kilnsey probably started as early as 1952. Climbers such as Arthur Dolphin, John Lockwood and Jack Bloor were amongst those who visited the crag, and Harold Drasdo and Keith King attempted to aid climb the route now known as Camelot. Joe Brown, Ron Moseley and members of the Rock and Ice visited Kilnsey in 1953 for an attempt on the Main Overhang but got no further than the roof at the time. It was not until 1957 that Moseley returned to complete his route, Original Route, and the following year Ron Hields and Ron Hirst linked Brown's first pitch with the Original Route to produce The Directissima at A3.

About this time, John Sumner and D. M. Adcock made an aided ascent of The Diedre. It was not freed until 1972 when Pete Livesey and John Sheard made their outstanding ascent, followed by the much harder (E4 6a) Central Wall to its left. The 1970s continued to see the elimination of aid points, but probably the most significant event was Livesey's ascent of Claws (E5 6a), a milepost in the history of free climbing at Kilnsey. Soon, more top climbers started to visit the crag. In 1980, Rob Gawthorpe freed the first pitch of The Directissima at E3 6a and followed it with Mistaken Identity at an incredible E4 7a with a near impossible series of starting moves. Ron Fawcett and the Berzins brothers were very active around this time, leaving many desperate calling cards. The pleasant Bird's Nest Crack was not discovered until the preparation of the 1985 YMC guide, *Yorkshire Limestone*, (ed., G. Desroy), its reasonable grade having been missed in the rush for the 'super routes'.

Progress has continued almost unabated, routes once the sole domain of the aid man now sprout shiny new bolts, and chalk dabs can be seen in the most unlikely places. Climbing standards are now at a level which would not have been believed even five years ago. No route is safe; in November 1988, Mark Leach free climbed the second pitch of The Directissima, the Main Overhang at E8 6c.

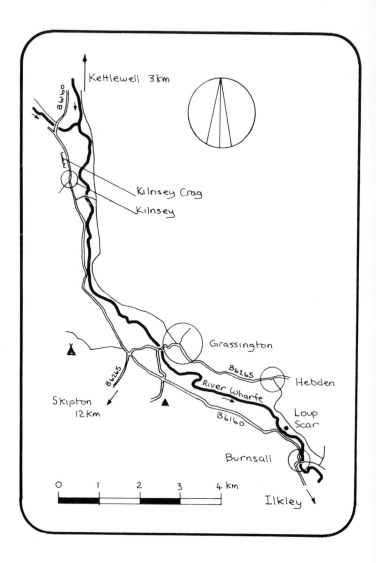

98: THE DIEDRE (E1) 50m

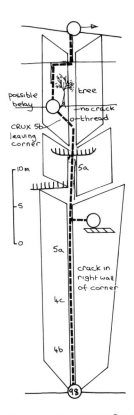

Summary: An essential outing taking the huge Diedre which runs the full height of the crag. A superb and classic free climb.

First Ascent: John Sumner and D. Adcock in 1956, using aid and climbed free by Pete Livesey and John Sheard in 1972.

Best Conditions: In the winter the whole of Kilnsey Crag can remain wet owing to seepage. The crag faces east and catches the morning sun and so the route usually is dry for the early summer.

Approach: *See* Approaches under Kilnsey Crag. Cross the wall and small stream and walk up to the crag.

Starting Point: At the foot of the obvious, huge open corner towards the right-hand end of the crag.

Descent: Either abseil from a tree close to the edge, 50m ropes just reach, or walk to the right (facing in) until you are past the farm, where an easy descent leads to the path at the foot of the crag.

The position on the second pitch is superb with views left across to Central Wall and other routes.

99: BIRD'S NEST CRACK (E1) 25m

Summary: A good line but somewhat overshadowed by its neighbours. Better and harder than it looks, it is well worth the effort.

First Ascent: Martin Berzins and Chris Sowden in 1984.

Best Conditions: This is a deep crack line leading into a vegetated gully and, as such, can remain damp for some time after a wet spell. However, the route usually remains dry for most of the early summer.

Approach: *See* Approaches under Kilnsey Crag. The route is in the central region of the crag, some 60m left of The Diedre and 30m left of the stone wall.

Starting Point: At the foot of the right-hand one of two well-defined crack systems.

Descent: By abseil from a large tree. The gully is not recommended.

Do not underestimate this easy-looking line; the crack is steeper than it looks and gives some absorbing climbing, particularly where the route rounds a small bulge and moves out onto the rib. One or two larger bits of gear might prove useful.

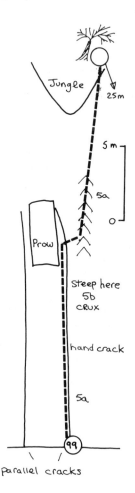

LOUP SCAR

A steep little crag which can be a real sun-trap when other buttresses are damp and cold, and far better than it appears from the opposite bank of the river. A must for the exhibitionist as the tourist path runs along the opposite bank with seats in the circle.

Approaches: Often good for a laugh or a wetting, Loup Scar is situated on the east (true left) bank of the River Wharfe, 500m upstream of the village of Burnsall, where there is ample car-parking space. The crag overhangs the river and, from Burnsall bridge, it is possible to walk up the true left bank and then scramble along the edge of the river to the crag. If the river is high, this approach is more difficult and involves some risk of drowning. Before the difficulties start, it is safer to follow small tracks which lead off to the right, up a bank to the top of the crag. From here it is possible to abseil in, having first ascertained that you are not abseiling into the river, unless of course you want to impress the tourists. In drought conditions it is possible to boulder hop from the more accessible right bank.

A Concise History: The history of the crag is concise. Loup Scar was first climbed on in 1964 by Paul Reinsch who climbed Central Crack as an aid route. Later, in 1968, Pete Livesey arrived to climb Louper, returning a couple of years later to add Lapper. Over the next few years, the crag was left neglected until, in 1984, Ron Fawcett visited the crag and free climbed the old aid route, Central Crack (E4). On the same visit, he added the adjacent roof problem Guadaloupe (E5 6b). Most of the remaining routes cross the roofs at E4 or E5 and were added by Martin Berzins, Chris Sowden and Paul Ingham during preparation for the YMC's 1985 guide *Yorkshire Limestone*.

An unknown climber on Beeston Eliminate (Route 83), Beeston Tor, Manifold Valley. (Photo: Chris Jackson.)

100: LAPPER & LOUPER (E2, E2)
22m, 22m

Summary: Two steep and exciting routes crossing unlikely territory, amongst a collection of large
roofs.

First Ascents: Louper and
Lapper – Pete Livesey, during the
late 1960s and early 1970s
respectively.

Best Conditions: The crag is so
overhanging that these routes can
remain dry when others in the area
are getting wet. Generally, the
routes are dry except after prolonged wet spells when they weep
and are slow to dry out. This is
another rock umbrella.

Approach: *See* Approaches under
Loup Scar.

Starting Point: Lapper – at the
foot of a pillar, below the left end of
the upper ramp. Louper – below a
thin crack in the bulging wall
towards the right end of the crag.

Descent: This is best by abseil
from one of the many trees along
the top of the crag. Ensure that you
are not abseiling into the river
which can be very deep and fast at
times. Alternatively, if the water is
low, walk downstream until it is possible to traverse in.

The unlikely nature of the two routes, set amongst a confusing maze of
overlapping roofs, is one of their several attractions. Both routes are steep
and strenuous and Lapper is particularly awkward at the start of the ramp,
where one is obliged to leave the security of some good protection.

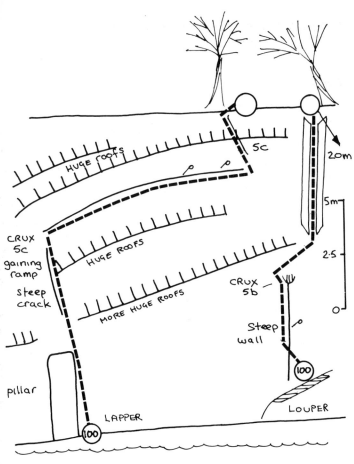

Also in the Crowood Classic Climbs Series:

Scotland
North Wales
Lake District
Yorkshire and The Peak District – Gritstone

EMERGENCIES

First Aid Checklist

Check Breathing
- If necessary, clear airway using a hooked finger to remove obstructions — vomit, blood, teeth etc.
- Unless a spinal injury is suspected, turn casualty to lie in the recovery position (on side). This helps to maintain a clear airway.

Check for Severe Bleeding
- Apply direct pressure from a pad to prevent bleeding.
- Elevate the limb.

Check for Broken Bones
- Do not move the casualty if a spinal injury is suspected.
- Immobilize other fractures using improvized splints or slings.

Monitor Condition
- Keep casualty warm and comfortable while waiting for rescue.
- Reassure casualty and monitor condition regularly.

To Alert Mountain Rescue
Dial 999, ask for police (mountain rescue) and try to have the following written details ready:

- Name and description of injured person.
- Precise location of injured person on crag.
- Location of crag (including *grid reference* and *map sheet number*).
- Time and nature of accident.
- Extent of injuries.
- Indication of prevailing weather at scene of accident (cloud base, wind strength, visibility etc.).
- Remain by the phone until met by a police officer or member of the rescue team.

Rescue Helicopters
- Secure all loose equipment before arrival of helicopter (weight loose objects with stones).
- Identify yourself by raising your arms in a V as helicopter approaches. Do *not* wave.
- Protect injured person from rotor downdraught which is intense).
- Allow winchman to land of his own accord.
- Do not approach helicopter unless directed to do so by one of the crew (danger from rotors, exhaust etc.).